The Flying Pizza
and Other Primary School Assemblies

The Flying Pizza
and Other Primary School Assemblies

Alan M. Barker

Edited by
Ronni Lamont

First published in Great Britain in 2014

Society for Promoting Christian Knowledge
36 Causton Street
London SW1P 4ST
www.spckpublishing.co.uk

British Library Cataloguing-in-Publication Data
A catalogue record for this book is available from the British Library

ISBN 978–0–281–07238–5

Typeset by Graphicraft Limited, Hong Kong
First printed in Great Britain by Ashford Colour Press
Subsequently digitally printed in Great Britain

Produced on paper from sustainable forests

CONTENTS

FOR ANY SEASON

Foreword

With these imaginative assemblies, we are clearly in the hands of a master. Alan Barker has a great gift for putting together a creative idea, a valuable message, uncomplicated props, lively participation and a fitting conclusion. In a moment, the teacher is almost there.

It's easy to fear that our own supply of suitable assemblies will dry up; Alan's never seem to. Schools all over the country have reason to be grateful to Alan for his constant flow of ideas. So, here they are – another set of oven-ready assemblies. They can be adapted, of course, but the hard work is already done.

Assemblies and Collective Worship are the times when a school is given its values. The core beliefs, the ethos – you might almost call it the *soul* of the school – is given shape on these occasions. Stories are told, ideas are explored, values are reinforced and beliefs are offered. They're worth taking time over – and that's when you need a friend like Alan Barker!

I know you'll enjoy browsing through this collection. You'll wish you could be a child again.

John Pritchard
Bishop of Oxford

Introduction

About 18 months ago, a friend came round for coffee. He had recently been ordained and had come direct from his first Harvest assembly at the local school. He was very happy. 'I did this amazing assembly that I found on your website,' he said. 'It's called "The flying pizza". Do you know the one I mean? It went down a storm!'

Indeed, I did know the one he meant. I used it myself when I was a parish priest for the Harvest celebration in church one year when I was running out of time and ideas. Why reinvent the wheel when you know the Assemblies website has this great assembly about pizzas?

Every year, 'The flying pizza' is one of our most popular assemblies for Harvest – even though it's been there since 2001. That means there are young people leaving school who experienced it early on and now another generation is taking part in this delightful, inspired exploration of one of our favourite foods. I sometimes comment that there can be few children in the country now who haven't experienced this assembly at some point in their lives!

Alan Barker, the author of 'The flying pizza', has the ability to come alongside children and explore the world that they live in, telling stories and delighting thousands of teachers, children and ministers who download his assemblies every year, as well as the schools that are part of his own ministerial round. He gently enables children's imaginations to take flight and so lets their spirituality come to the fore.

Thus, we felt it was time to dedicate a whole book to the writer of 'The flying pizza'. Of course, 'The flying pizza' is here, together with other tried and tested assemblies and 30 new ones, to enable you to work with children in your school or group, enjoying and exploring together. 'The flying pizza' itself has been slightly edited, to bring it up to date, and, if you've never used it, do – it's never too late!

Ronni Lamont
Editor
www.assemblies.org.uk

AUTUMN

THE FLYING PIZZA
Harvest

Suitable for Whole School

 Aim

To appreciate the scale of global food production and the concept of 'food miles'.

 Preparation and materials

- You will need the ingredients to make a pizza – a pizza base, tomato passata or purée, sliced beef tomato, sliced red onion, sliced red and/or green pepper, drained tinned pineapple chunks, drained tinned sweetcorn, sliced mushrooms, grated Mozzarella cheese, freshly ground black pepper. Also, if possible, arrange to be able to cook and share the pizza.
- Create some images to convey the distances travelled for each of the ingredients for the pizza and have the means to display them during the assembly. The distances need only be approximate and the countries of origin of the ingredients may vary according to the season, so adapt as appropriate. See the examples given in the 'Assembly', Step 2, below.
- You could, if you wish, arrange for a group of children to present other examples of locally bought but globally produced food, such as tea, coffee, fruit, which would increase involvement and extend the learning.

 Assembly

1. Explain that, when you are feeling hungry, it's sometimes a nice treat to order a takeaway pizza. Tell the children the distance to the local pizza takeaway and how, for many people, a pizza can be cooked and delivered in a short time.

2. Introduce the idea that the ingredients used to make the pizza might have travelled much further. Explain by inviting a group of children to help place the toppings on to the prepared pizza base. As the pizza is made, display the images showing the distances the different ingredients have travelled. These might include, for example:
   - the flour to make the base, from Canadian wheat   3300 miles
   - tomato passata or purée, from Italy (the home of pizzas)   900 miles
   - beef tomato, from Morocco   1300 miles
   - red onion, grown in the United Kingdom   200 miles
   - pineapple, grown in Kenya   4500 miles
   - peppers, grown in Spain   900 miles
   - mushrooms, grown in Holland   300 miles
   - sweetcorn, produced in Thailand   6000 miles
   - Mozzarella cheese, also from Italy   900 miles
   - black peppercorns, from India   4200 miles

   So the pizza that is delivered from 'just around the corner' has, in fact, flown an incredible distance of 22,500 miles around the world.

3. Remind the children that much of the food we take for granted has been produced in other parts of the world, travelling great distances to reach our plates. Encourage them to look at the labels of tins and packets as they shop.

If the option of having a group of children present other examples of locally bought but globally produced food has been chosen, they should do so at this point.

4. For Key Stage 2 children, introduce the concept of 'food miles' and explain that this means the distance food is transported from producers to 'consumers' (those who buy and eat it). Modern transport and refrigeration enables us to enjoy food from all around the world, at school, in our homes and restaurants. The downside of this, however, is that much fuel is burned to bring those foods to us in airplanes and lorries, at a cost to both consumers and the environment.

5. Encourage everyone to use the occasion of a Harvest celebration to think about the varied origins of our food and the benefits and disadvantages of food that 'travels miles'.

6. Cook and enjoy the 'flying' pizza!

 Time for reflection

We must not take for granted the ability of the Earth to grow food. There is always the danger that, with plentiful food supplies, we won't stop to think how much we depend on others.

> *Prayer*
> Creator God,
> Thank you for food from around the world and for the different tastes that we enjoy.
> Help us to use the resources of the Earth wisely and well, to the benefit of all people.
> **Amen.**

 Songs

'Lord of the harvest' (*Come and Praise*, 133)

'Harvest samba' (*Songs for Every Occasion*, Out of the Ark Music, 2002)

ACHIEVING THE IMPOSSIBLE
New school year/new term

Suitable for Whole School

Aim

To appreciate the need for perseverance to achieve ideals.

Preparation and materials

- You will need a leader, if possible wearing a pair of trainers and tracksuit, and eight children, dressed for running, each with a letter on their backs, together spelling the word 'marathon'. The children need to prepare so that they can make the responses set out in the 'Assembly', Step 1, below.
- You will also need another reader to say the short passage from 2 Timothy 4.7 in Step 9.

Assembly

1. *Leader*: *Introduce the theme by running on the spot, together with the team of eight children (who are in order, so as to spell 'marathon' when they turn their backs to the audience), and have the following conversation with them.*

   Leader: How long can you run on the spot? Three minutes?

   Children: Yes!

   Leader: What about three hours?

   Children: Three hours?!

   Leader: I'm getting tired.

   Children: Don't give up!

   Leader: How far can you run? Twice around the playground?

   Children: Yes!

   Leader: What about 26 miles?

   Children: 26 miles?!

   Leader: I'm getting tired.

   Children: Don't give up!

2. *Leader*: There's a race that's over 26 miles long. It would take you at least three hours to finish. Even the best runners take over two hours. It's called . . .

   Children turn their backs to the audience to reveal the letters

   . . . a marathon!

3. *All stop jogging.* Ask if any of the children watched the London Marathon on television (or a local race). What impressed them most?

4. Think about the crowds who cheer the runners on, saying, 'Don't give up'. Talk about the tired runners, who must have felt their legs wobbling as they neared the end of the course. Knowing that they hadn't got far to go, they didn't give up.

5. Talk about other runners (some in fancy dress) who were raising money for their chosen charities. It must have been hot inside those heavy costumes, but the thought of those they were helping meant that they didn't give up!

6. Point out that wheelchair athletes compete in the marathon. Injuries and disability are not reasons to give up!

7. Explain that the London Marathon was first held in 1981, after a man called Chris Brasher took part in a marathon in New York. Sadly, he has passed away, but at the time, after completing the marathon, he wrote of his experience, saying, 'To believe this story, you must believe that the human race can be one joyous family, working together, laughing together, achieving the impossible.'

8. The London and other marathons demonstrate that little is achieved without perseverance. In order to run so far, training is vital. That means jogging regularly for many months before the race. It involves running increasingly longer distances once a week, until 26 miles is reached. Perseverance means spending long hours exercising and practising before the race itself. Both during the training and the race itself, you mustn't give up!

9. Explain that marathons were run in the Greek games, centuries ago, at the time of Jesus, and were known to Paul. Paul's letters are in the Bible. He wrote words of encouragement, saying (2 Timothy 4.7, GNB):

    Reader: I have done my best in the race, I have run the full distance, and I have kept the faith.

    Leader: To put it more simply, 'Whatever I've done, I've not given up!'

10. Invite the children to consider the challenges the new school year/a new term presents. There are many other things we do, besides running, that are not easy. Many tasks require practice and commitment. Can the children think of examples? A marathon reminds us that, together, we can help and encourage one another. We can achieve things that seem impossible, if we don't give up!

 Time for reflection

Ask the children to think about how hard it must be to run a marathon. Ask them to think, too, about what difficult tasks face them this term or year. How could they encourage one another?

> *Prayer*
> Dear God,
> Give us strength of body, mind and spirit, to face new challenges, to keep trying and to realize our potential.
> **Amen.**

 Song

'One more step along the world I go' (*Come and Praise*, 47)

A HARVEST RAINBOW

Suitable for Whole School

 Aim

To celebrate the different colours, shapes and tastes of harvest fruits.

 Preparation and materials

- You will need a variety of fruits, reflecting the colours of the rainbow, such as:
  - for red – bowl of strawberries and a red apple
  - for orange – satsumas or clementines and a larger orange
  - for yellow – honeydew melon, a banana and a lemon
  - for green – large green cooking and Granny Smith apples, perhaps a kiwi fruit
  - for blue or indigo – blueberries on a blue dish
  - for purple – black grapes and dark plums.
- You will also need a table of suitable height to use for display, covered with a blue cloth.
- Create an image with the words 'A Harvest Rainbow' and a photograph or drawing of a rainbow on it, plus the text of Genesis 8.22, if required, and have the means available to display it during the assembly.

 Assembly

1. Introduce the assembly by saying that you have brought a rainbow to add to the harvest display. It's not the kind of rainbow that you might see in the sky, but one that has the same variety of colours. This rainbow is very special because, unlike real rainbows, you can touch and even taste it! It's a harvest rainbow.

2. Ask the children to help make the rainbow appear. Explain that the first colour of a rainbow is red. Invite them to identify some red fruit and begin to create the display on the table by asking the children to place some strawberries together with the red apple on the blue cloth, at the bottom left corner.

   Continue with the oranges, melon, banana, lemon, green apples and so on, placing them in colour order so that the harvest rainbow forms. Comment that few fruits are coloured blue or indigo, but introduce the dish of blueberries and, finally, two different shades of purple with the grapes and plums.

3. As you do this, take time to introduce the fruits in turn. Note their different shapes and sizes. With older children, discuss where and how are they grown.

4. Reflect that the harvest rainbow is bright *and* healthy! Fruit is good for us to eat. It contains the fresh vitamins and fibre needed to keep our bodies strong and well.

5. In a church school, you could go on to explain that, at harvest time, Christians remember the rainbow that appears in the story of Noah.

   Display the image with the rainbow created as described in the 'Preparation and materials' section above.

   That rainbow was a sign of God's care for the world. It spoke of the patterns of nature and people remembered an age-old promise God made (Genesis 8.22, GNB):

As long as the world exists, there will be a time for planting and a time for harvest. There will always be cold and heat, summer and winter, day and night.

6. Observe that the harvest rainbow celebrates the good things of life, which are for us to enjoy. The 'colours of the rainbow' fill the world around us. Do we take time to see and appreciate them?

7. Finally, reflect that eventually all rainbows disappear. Explain that this might happen to this rainbow, too, if we make a fruit salad to taste the different colours of the harvest rainbow!

 Time for reflection

Prayer

Creator God,
Today we are thankful for . . .
the rainbow colours of your world
brilliant fruit that is good to eat
the light of day and the darkness of night
the beauty of the changing seasons
nature's patterns of seedtime and harvest.
Thank you!
Amen.

 Songs

'All things bright and beautiful' (*Come and Praise*, 3)

'Pears and apples' (*Come and Praise*, 135)

'Food colours' (*A Combined Harvest*, Out of the Ark Music, 2008)

'Juicy fruit' (*Sing Harvest*, Out of the Ark Music, 2012)

A HARVEST YOU CAN COUNT ON

Suitable for Whole School

 Aim

To retell the parable of the sower to celebrate generosity.

 Preparation and materials

- You will need some grains and a few stems of wheat (pet shops, healthfood shops and florists can be good sources of these), one small and ten large potatoes, a dozen or so pods of peas or runner beans with a few of their seeds, plus a large marrow or pumpkin (the last item is optional).
- Familiarize yourself with the story told in the 'Assembly' below, rehearsing the actions indicated to accompany it or helping some children to mime it while it is being told. Note that the phrase and finger action '30 times, 60 times, 100 times' is to be a catchphrase for everyone during this assembly.

 Assembly

1. Show the children the grains of wheat and invite them to listen to a story Jesus told about generosity – explaining that 'generosity' means 'giving freely'.

   The parable of the sower

   Once there was a man who went into his field to sow seeds. He flung out his arms, letting the seed run through his fingers. *(Sowing action.)*

   Some seed fell along the path. *(Flat hand movements.)* The birds came and ate it up. *(Link thumbs and flap fingers.)*

   Some seed fell into rocky soil. The plants began to grow. *(Raise arms and form branches and leaves with hands and stay in this position.)* Sadly, the rocky soil stopped the roots from finding water. When the sun grew hot, the plants quickly withered away. *(Hands tremble and arms droop to sides.)*

   Some seed fell among thorns *(go to touch and recoil as if touching something spiky)*, which grew up and choked the plants.

   Some seed fell into good soil, where it grew well. *(Lift hands and arms up, as if growing.)*

   It produced a good harvest – 30 times, 60 times, 100 times. *(Triumphantly display three, six and ten fingers.)*

   You may wish to repeat the story, inviting everyone to join in with the actions. Then show the children the stems of wheat and invite them to consider what '30 times, 60 times, 100 times' means. It's a way of saying that one tiny seed can produce a harvest of many grains.

   Observe that the story also describes how the sower was generous. He worked very hard and sowed lots of seeds, even though he knew some would be wasted.

   Note how generosity brings a harvest we can count on *(say it all together and do the actions)* 30 times, 60 times, 100 times!

2. Describe how this can be true of our own experiences of growing vegetables. One small potato *(show small potato)* is put into the ground and, later in the year, ten or more can be lifted from underneath the plant. *(Count the large potatoes together, one by one.)*

In the meantime, they must be kept weeded and watered. This requires patience and can be hard work, but the time and generosity we give the seeds brings a harvest you can count on *(say it all together and do the actions)* 30 times, 60 times, 100 times!

Reflect how a seed pea or bean grows to produce many pods. *(Show the pods and count them together one by one.)* Open a mature pod to find the peas or beans inside. How many are there?

Lots of compost must be dug into the soil to grow these crops. They, too, must be watered. It's hard work, but the time and generosity given brings a harvest you can count on *(say it all together and do the actions)* 30 times, 60 times, 100 times!

Produce the large marrow or pumpkin (if using) and say, 'There's generosity!' *(then say it all together and do the actions)* 30 times, 60 times, 100 times!

3. Reflect that, at harvest time, we celebrate the generosity of nature. We also focus on the hard work and generosity of those who grow our crops. So, we must say 'Thank you' for a harvest we can count on *(say it all together and do the actions)* 30 times, 60 times, 100 times!

 Time for reflection

Prayer

Creator God,
Thank you for seeds that yield a harvest
30 times, 60 times, 100 times!
We remember those whose hard work helps the harvest to grow.
May we say 'Thank you', not just once, but
30 times, 60 times, 100 times!

 Songs

'Harvest song' (*Songs for Every Season*, Out of the Ark Music, 1997)

'For the harvest' (*Sing Harvest*, Out of the Ark Music, 2012)

'We plough the fields and scatter' (*Hymns Old and New* (Kevin Mayhew), 801, 2008 edition)

UNDERGROUND, OVERGROUND
Harvest

Suitable for Key Stage 1

 Aim

To celebrate and enjoy vegetables and the different ways in which they are grown and harvested.

 Preparation and materials

- You will need a wide range of vegetables, preferably loose rather than prepacked, such as carrot and beetroot (with or without tops), radish, potato, swede, leek, onion, cabbage, cauliflower, lettuce, cucumber, tomato, whole ear of corn on the cob, pepper, spinach, marrow, pumpkin or squash, runner bean. Set them out attractively on a table for the assembly, ensuring that the children will be able to see them.
- Throughout the assembly have fun by using a thumbs down sign to signify 'underground' and thumbs up for 'overground'.
- Have available some appropriate images of harvesting and the means to display them during the assembly (check copyright).

 Assembly

1. Refer to the display of vegetables and reflect that one of the joys of harvest is the colourful and varied appearance of the foods that we eat. Not only do vegetables look and taste different but they also grow and are gathered in different ways.

2. Explain that the seeds of all vegetables are sown in the soil, but, as the plants grow, some of the vegetables develop as roots and tubers hidden underground, while others become leaves, pods and fruit that grow above the surface, or overground.

   Select some of the vegetables. Identify them with the children. Invite the children to respond to the question each time as to whether the bits we eat can be found, 'Underground or overground?' Ask them to use a thumbs up gesture to indicate overground or a thumbs down gesture for underground.

3. Describe the various patterns of growth. For example, potatoes must be 'earthed up' in ridges to help the crop grow without any light reaching them. Runner beans need the support of poles that they cling to and, when they do, they can grow fast! Some crops, such as carrots, may need to be 'thinned out', so that the roots have room to grow.

4. Explain the different ways in which vegetables are harvested. Underground crops need to be harvested from the ground. So, potatoes are dug up and separated from the plant or haulm. Carrots and other root crops are pulled – perhaps after the ground has been loosened with a fork.

   Overground crops don't need to be dug up as they are helpfully above the soil. So, cabbages, cauliflowers, lettuce and marrows are cut from the stem. Peppers and tomatoes, beans and sweetcorn are picked from the plant.

5. Which vegetables do the children like best? Are they underground or overground ones? Reflect that some of the most enjoyable meals can be those with both underground *and* overground vegetables mixed on the plate. At harvest, then, we are thankful for both. Show the children one thumb down and the other up and get them to join in with you.

6. Sing the following song to the tune of 'Polly put the kettle on', with appropriate harvesting actions.

Sing a song of harvest time
Sing a song of harvest time
Sing a song of carrots *(thumbs down)*
We pull to eat.

Sing a song of harvest time
Sing a song of harvest time
Sing a song of cabbages *(thumbs up)*
We cut to eat.

Sing a song of harvest time
Sing a song of harvest time
Sing of a song of potatoes *(thumbs down)*
We dig to eat.

Sing a song of harvest time
Sing a song of harvest time
Sing a song of peppers *(thumbs up)*
We pick to eat.

(This song can be carried on, with individual children suggesting or holding up different vegetables. It could be concluded with the following verse.)

Thank you, Lord, for harvest time
Thank you, Lord, for harvest time
Underground and overground
For us to eat.

Time for reflection

Adapt the following prayer according to your vegetables. Invite everyone to join in with saying 'Thank you' when this phrase is said in the prayer.

Prayer

Creator God,
We want to say 'Thank you' for the vegetables we enjoy.
For tiny seeds that grow into huge marrows, we say
'Thank you.'
For runner beans hanging like icicles,
'Thank you.'
For bright red radishes and deep purple beetroot,
'Thank you.'
For leafy green cabbages growing in rows,
'Thank you.'
For bright orange carrots hidden in the earth,
'Thank you.'
For red tomatoes ripening slowly in the sun,
'Thank you.'
For harvest that is underground and overground,
'Thank you.'

Song

'The singing vegetables' (*Sing Harvest*, Out of the Ark Music, 2012)

FACING YOUR FEARS
Hallowe'en

Suitable for Whole School

 Aim

To help children become more sensitive to the fears and feelings of others.

 Preparation and materials

- You will need a large pumpkin, kept hidden until required.
- An empty lidded box will serve as the 'mood box' for the drama exercise.
- Familiarize yourself with the stories in Luke 8 and the simple retellings given in the 'Assembly', Step 5, below (optional).

 Assembly

1. Ask the children to think back (or forwards, depending on the time of year) to Hallowe'en – a festival when many people have fun.

2. Uncover the pumpkin. Is anyone surprised? How can we tell from people's faces?

3. Refer to the tradition of carving a face by hollowing out a pumpkin. What kind of face should it be? Friendly or fierce?

4. Invite the children to consider how their faces can reveal their feelings. Explain how actors use facial expressions to convey the feelings of their characters.

5. Hold a fun warm-up session. Show the 'mood box' and challenge individual children to open the box and respond to the imaginary contents by showing different emotions – making fierce, frightened, sad, happy, disgusted, surprised, puzzled or friendly faces. Can the others guess the mood from the child's face?

6. If including, retell the following stories from Luke 8 to the children and invite them to enter into the feelings of the characters – first, Jesus' frightened and amazed friends, then the aggression of Legion, finishing with everyone's smiles of relief. Encourage them to participate using appropriate facial expressions. Assume the role of Jesus as you tell the story with authority and sensitivity.

The look on their faces

I shall always remember the look on their faces. We'd had a really busy day and I suggested that we should borrow a boat and sail across the Sea of Galilee to find a peaceful spot. My friends all nodded and smiled.

'Good idea,' they said.

I was so tired I fell asleep on the boat. How was I to know a fierce storm was coming? The wind blew like a hurricane, the boat rocked to and fro, but it didn't wake me. My friends woke me, though. For a moment, I wondered what was wrong. I could see they were terrified.

'Don't you care? We're going to drown!' they screamed.

I stood up and said, 'Peace, be still.' The wind began to die down and the waves became calm and my friends, who were still shaking, looked surprised and puzzled. They exclaimed, 'Wow! What was all that about?'

When we got to shore, we met another storm – one in someone's mind. First we heard strange cries and banging noises. Then we found a man living among the rocks and caves. He shouted and made fierce faces at us. He was very ill.

People shook their heads. They told us that he ran around like an animal. They had tried to help him, but didn't know how. Everyone was very frightened of him.

When he saw that we weren't frightened, Legion (that was the man's name) came across to us. We talked and, gradually, his face became gentler and the wild look disappeared from his eyes. I told him to go to his friends to explain that he was better. I knew that wouldn't be difficult – you could tell it from his face. I could tell from his friends' faces that they were pleased, too!

7. Conclude by inviting everyone to become more aware of the feelings of others – by looking at their faces and remembering that a smile can give others so much help and encouragement.

8. What of Hallowe'en or other times when we sense that people are becoming nervous or even frightened? Reflect that it can be fun to face our fears, but, if it is obvious from their faces that anyone (especially the old or very young) is really frightened, then don't be a fierce pumpkin . . . be sensitive to how others feel.

 Time for reflection

We like to be scared – sometimes. A spooky story, a scary film, perhaps a dare can be fun for some, but we don't all feel the same. Your 'fun' may be someone else's fear; their 'joke' may be your fear!

Prayer
Loving God,
May your love and strength be felt in our hearts
and shown on our faces,
today and every day.
Amen.

 Song

'Peace is flowing like a river' (*Come and Praise*, 144)

BREAKING DOWN THE WALL
Fall of the Berlin Wall (9 November 1989)

Suitable for Key Stage 2

 Aim

To reflect on aspects of political and personal freedom.

 Preparation and materials

- Some sheets with which to form a 'wall'.
- Enlist the help of some older children or colleagues to hold the sheets taut and a couple of colleagues to take charge of each side of the 'wall' during the assembly. Arrange, too, for them to echo what you say in the 'Assembly', Step 9, below.
- Find some images of the Berlin Wall and have the means to display them during the assembly (check copyright). The Berlin Wall fell on 9 November 1989.
- Have available the song 'Something inside so strong' by Labi Siffre and the means to play it while the children come in and sit down and as they leave the assembly. Alternatively, 'Pressure points' or 'West Berlin' by Camel (check copyright).

 Assembly

1. Explain that this assembly explores the theme of freedom. It marks a time, in 1989, when the people of Berlin, now the capital of Germany, regained freedoms that had been denied to them by the building of a wall.

   State that, to help everyone understand some of the problems of that time, you have decided to divide the school.

2. Ask that a gap be formed down the centre of the gathered children, separating the classes in half.

   Call on your helpers to build a 'wall' in the gap using the sheets. Screen the two halves from each other and place a colleague in charge of each side.

3. How does the division feel? Explore the feelings of uncertainty and discomfort that may arise. What is going on? Who is on the other side of the wall?

4. Explain that, after the Second World War, Germany was divided into two parts like this and the city of Berlin was split into East and West sections. East and West had very different systems of government and they had deep mistrust and suspicion of each other.

5. In August 1961, the citizens woke to street crossing points blocked by barriers and barbed wire. The authorities in the East had decided to stop people crossing to other parts of the city. Later, a high concrete wall was built. It was protected with barbed wire and watched by armed guards. Invite everyone to imagine how the citizens of Berlin must have felt.

6. Designate one half of the assembly as 'East' and the other as 'West'. Invite the children to enter into further role play. State that those in the 'East' will not be allowed to use the playground. New classes will have to be formed. Those in the East will not be permitted to join after-school or lunchtime clubs and they will not be allowed representatives on the School Council.

Those in the West will also be grouped into new classes, but, otherwise, for them school will carry on as normal. They will be free to use the playground and take part in clubs and elect members of the School Council. Sometimes they might ask permission to visit a classroom belonging to a group from the East, but under no circumstances will anyone from the East be allowed to visit the West. Neither is a visit from West to East guaranteed – you will have to apply and may be refused permission. Any person who breaks this rule will be punished!

7. Reassure the children that this is 'make-believe', but invite them to reflect on how they would feel if such directions were given. How would each group respond? Explore how a dividing wall would affect friendships, family relationships and day-to-day life.

8. Reflect that the Berlin Wall separated friends and families. Some were unable to travel to their usual places of work. Those living in East Berlin were not allowed the choices and freedoms enjoyed by those in the West. Protest was not permitted and anyone who tried to escape across the wall was shot. Above all, those in the East were not allowed to elect (choose) their leaders or express their views freely and openly.

   For years, the wall divided the city. No one was sure whether or not or how anything could change.

9. Eventually, it became possible for a few in the East to say, 'Down with the wall!' *(A few of your helpers on the East side repeat this phrase.)* Soon, other voices joined in the protest. Eventually, large crowds gathered in the streets, all shouting, 'Down with the wall!' *(Invite more and more on the East side to participate.)*

   It was a dangerous thing to do. No one knew how the authorities would react – perhaps with anger and violence. People climbed up on the wall and hammered at it with sledgehammers and chisels – the crowds cheered. Then, on 9 November 1989, the wall 'fell'. *(Instruct your helpers to drop the 'wall'.)*

   The checkpoints in the wall were opened for those in the East to go through to the West! Thousands of people celebrated late into the night. They danced, joined hands and hugged each other with joy! After almost 30 years, East and West were reunited. Bulldozers were soon continuing the demolition work that had been started with hammers and chisels! A new chapter in history had begun.

10. How does everyone feel now that they are reunited? Reflect that the story of the Berlin Wall helps us to think about some of the freedoms we take for granted. It reminds us of the importance of working together for peace and unity.

 Time for reflection

From the Christian tradition, a letter written by Paul to the Ephesians (2.14, *The Message*) says:

> *He tore down the wall we used to keep each other at a distance.*

Give the children time to reflect on their feelings during this assembly. Remind them that the wall was in place for 27 years – that's longer than some of the teachers have been alive! Since the wall came down, life in Germany has changed for everyone, in both the East and the West.

Reflect for a few moments on the thought that the cost of freedom is sometimes not anticipated or fully understood.

Prayer

God of all humanity,
often people are separated by
ambition and greed,
anger and fear,
arrogance and pride.
Help us to break down walls of division and misunderstanding
and celebrate that we belong together,
citizens of one world.
Amen.

 Song

'Let the world rejoice' (*Come and Praise*, 148)

ARMISTICE DAY (11 NOVEMBER)

Suitable for Key Stage 2

Aim

To consider the significance of 11 November, Armistice Day.

Preparation and materials

- This assembly can be used on or prior to 11 November, in preparation for the observance of the two minutes' silence.
- It may be helpful to display the words 'Armistice Day' and the Latin words from which the word 'armistice' is derived – 'arma' (weapons) and 'sistere' (to stop).
- You could read the short poem 'The Cherry Trees' by Edward Thomas, which is available at <www.poemhunter.com/poem/the-cherry-trees> (optional).

Assembly

1. Note that 11 November is often referred to as Armistice Day. Explain that the word 'armistice' comes from two Latin words, 'arma', meaning 'weapons', and 'sistere', meaning 'to stop'. 'An armistice' is a truce, an agreement to stop fighting – to be still.

2. The eleventh day of November is known as Armistice Day because this was the day, in 1918, when the First World War (or Great War) ended. It was agreed that the fighting should stop on the 'eleventh hour of the eleventh day of the eleventh month'.

3. The First World War started in 1914. In a little over four years, over 8.5 million people died worldwide and another 20 million were injured. Such was the loss of life that, in almost every village and town, there were many men who never returned from the fighting.

4. *If including 'The Cherry Trees' poem, say the following.*

   This tragedy is reflected in a short poem by Edward Thomas called 'The Cherry Trees'. The poet was one of those eventually killed in the war.

   Read the poem and invite the children to respond to it.

   In the poem, Edward Thomas pictures the lovely sight of springtime blossom scattered along a country road, the fallen petals looking like wedding confetti, but a feeling of sadness dims the joy of spring. This is the road along which men had marched as they left to fight in France and now they have been lost. One of the consequences of the Great War was that large numbers of women were unable to marry – so many men had died, making the image of wedding confetti doubly sad.

5. In 1919, King George V asked that people remember and honour all those who had died in the service of their country. Two minutes' silence was held at 11 o'clock on the eleventh day of the eleventh month. A year after the war ended, it was not guns that stopped being fired, but busy streets and traffic that stood still on Armistice Day. Today, 100 years later, Armistice Day continues to be a time to remember those who have died in war.

6. Sadly, the Great War was not, as some people at the time hoped it would be, the 'war to end all wars'. On this anniversary, we also remember all the people who have died during military service since 1918 – in the Second World War, the Gulf War and Afghanistan, for example.

7. Outline how the two minutes' silence will be observed by the school community. It will be a time for everyone to stop what they are doing and stand still. Ask the children what they will feel and think during that time. Suggest that various thoughts and emotions may be felt:
   - the sadness and sorrow that war brings
   - gratitude for the work of those who serve in the armed forces
   - a feeling of pride and of belonging
   - a strong sense of the need to work and pray for peace.

8. Church schools may wish to also refer to a verse from Psalm 46: 'Be still, and know that I am God!' (verse 10). Being and standing still can help us to think about things that are very important.

 Time for reflection

A time of silence could be introduced by reading 'The Cherry Trees' if it was not read in the 'Assembly', Step 4, above or by simply saying, 'Let us be still and remember.'

It might be concluded with the traditional words of the Ode of Remembrance:

Leader: At the going down of the sun, and in the morning, we will remember them.
All: **We will remember them.**

 Song

'Make me a channel of your peace' (*Come and Praise*, 147)

WINTER

GETTING STIRRED UP!
Week preceding Advent

Suitable for Whole School

Aim

To mix a Christmas pudding while sharing hopes and aspirations for a better world.

Preparation and materials

- You will need a large glass mixing bowl and a wooden spoon.
- You will also need the following Christmas pudding ingredients, weighed separately, each kept in its own food bag, ready for the assembly:
  - 75 g currants
  - 75 g sultanas
  - 75 g raisins
  - 50 g mixed peel
  - 25 g glacé cherries
  - 85 g soft brown sugar
  - 85 g suet
  - 100 g fresh breadcrumbs
  - 1 tablespoon self-raising flour
  - $\frac{1}{2}$ teaspoon ground mixed spice
  - 2 medium eggs
  - 1 apple, can be grated and added later to moisten mix.
- Ensure that there will be a table or other surface on which to set out your equipment and the ingredients during the assembly.
- Prepare the stir up prayer in the 'Time for reflection' section below for display.

Assembly

1. *Set up the table, bowl, spoon and ingredients before the children arrive for the assembly.*

   Explain that the Sunday before Advent is known as 'Stir up Sunday'. The name comes from the tradition of mixing Christmas puddings on that Sunday. Establish that 'a tradition' is something done year after year on a certain date or occasion.

2. Describe how, according to the tradition, families mix the pudding together so that each member of the family can make a Christmas wish. Ask the children, 'What would be your Christmas wish, not just for yourself but also for others? How might the world be made a better place for everyone?'

   Allow the children a few moments for reflection, then invite some of them to share their hopes, stir the pudding and also, perhaps, secretly make a wish for themselves!

3. As hopes are shared, add the ingredients to the bowl one by one, helping the children as necessary to stir them together. It's important to keep the assembly itself stirred up and moving, too! Affirm and reflect back the hopes to link and develop strands of thought. Contributions might relate to concerns about care and friendship, the BBC's Children in Need Appeal, items of world news and environmental issues.

4. When all the ingredients have been added and stirred together, explain that the next stage is to allow the mixture to stand overnight. A little orange juice can be added if needed before the mixture is transferred into smaller bowls, wrapped tightly in foil and steamed or boiled in a slow-cooker for eight hours. The puddings will then keep until Christmas. Many changes we long for, like Christmas puddings, may take time, but we need to remember and hold on to our hopes!

5. Conclude with a word of encouragement to those who have not been able to participate. Maybe their turn will come should the tradition be followed next year!

 Time for reflection

Show the children the display version of the following prayer you created and mention that it is based on a prayer traditionally said for Stir up Sunday. Invite everyone to spend a few moments focusing on the hopes that have been shared and say the prayer together.

> *Prayer*
> Lord God,
> Stir us up,
> to think how we can help others,
> share the fruits of friendship,
> and make life rich and rewarding.
> **Amen.**

 Songs

'Give us hope, Lord' (*Come and Praise*, 87)

'Today' (*Songs for Every Assembly*, Out of the Ark Music, 1999)

LET'S ALL GO TO BETHLEHEM
Christmas

Suitable for Whole School

 Aim

To enter into the experience of the shepherds and demonstrate that fears can be overcome.

 Preparation and materials

- Familiarize yourself with the story and actions in the 'Assembly', Step 3, below, so that you can focus on making it expressive and compelling.
- Read the story of the shepherds in Luke 2.8–16. An accessible version of this can be read in the 'Assembly', Step 2, but is optional.
- A lit candle can be used as a focus during the 'Time for reflection' section of the assembly, if wished.

 Assembly

1. Ask the children, 'Have you ever been afraid of the dark?' Acknowledge that many people feel uncomfortable and frightened in darkness. At night it's difficult to see. Obstacles cause us to stumble and fall. Noises are startling. Reflect that, away from city streetlights and homes, the open countryside can seem very dark and frightening.

2. Refer to the story of the first Christmas. Shepherds stayed on the hills throughout the night, watching and guarding their flocks. Their only light was perhaps the glow of a fire. They were terrified when they saw an angel, but, after seeing Jesus, they no longer felt afraid.

   Read the passage from Luke 2.8–16 at this point, if you wish.

3. Invite the children to imagine that they are with the shepherds on their journey to Bethlehem. Encourage them to quickly echo your words *and* actions, which will work best if delivered with appropriate pace and a sense of fun.

   Let's all go to Bethlehem

   Let's all go to Bethlehem. *(Beckon.)*

   We've seen an angel! *(Raised arms.)*

   And heard about a baby, *(arms as if cradling a baby)*

   a very special baby. *(Nod knowingly.)*

   Leave the sheep behind. Baa!

   It's so dark! *(Look around nervously.)*

   So very cold! *(Shiver.)*

   Are you frightened? *(Nod head for 'Yes'.)*

   All together then. *(Motion to others.)*

   Quickly down the hill. Follow me! *(Stride on the spot.)*

   Across the stream. Splish, splash. *(Make small leaps.)*

   Through the prickly bushes. Ow! Ouch! Ow! *(Flinch in pain.)*

Look at that brilliant star. Wow! *(Point upwards.)*

Stop! There's a stable. *(Stand still.)*

Push open the door. *(Push and peer around edge of door.)*

Tiptoe in quietly. *(Tiptoe.)*

Peep into the manger. *(Lean over and look downwards.)*

He's asleep! *(Index finger on lips.)*

Don't wake the baby. *(Whispered.)*

Tiptoe out softly. *(Tiptoe.)*

Close the door gently. *(Pull door to.)*

A baby has been born! Let's all jump for joy! *(Jump for joy!)*

It's just as the angels promised! Let's all shout hurray! *(Shout 'Hurray!')*

His name is Jesus! Let's tell the others! *(Beckon.)*

All together then. *(Motion to others.)*

Through the prickly bushes. Ow! Ouch! Ow! *(Flinch in pain.)*

Across the stream. Splish, splash. *(Make small leaps.)*

Quickly up the hill. Follow me! *(Stride on the spot.)*

Back to the sheep. Baa!

It's so dark. *(Look around.)*

So very cold. *(Shiver.)*

Are you frightened? *(Shake head for 'No'.)*

No! Not at all. *(Smile.)*

We've seen the special baby! *(Arms as if cradling a baby.)*

4. Conclude by saying that the Christmas story tells how faith in God can help to overcome fear. The shepherds returned to their flocks with joy and confidence.

 Time for reflection

Spend some moments thinking of anyone who may be afraid tonight.

If you are afraid, remember that there are others who understand how you feel.

The following affirmation of faith may also be repeated a phrase at a time.

Prayer
Jesus is born! *(Light the candle, if using.)*
Light in the darkness.
Peace be with you!

 Song

Christmas carol, such as 'Away in a manger' or 'How far is it to Bethlehem?'

RUMOURS OF RUDOLPH
Christmas

Suitable for Whole School

 Aim

To reflect on the meaning of Christmas good will.

 Preparation and materials

- You will need a pair of Christmas reindeer antlers.
- Ahead of the assembly, arrange with two or more colleagues what you are going to say, along the lines given in the 'Assembly', Step 2, below.
- Have available the song and lyrics for 'Rudolph the red-nosed reindeer' and the means to play it during the assembly. Familiarize yourself with the accompanying actions.
- A play or dance could be written to illustrate the song.

 Assembly

1. Put on the party antlers and tell the children that you're really getting into the spirit of Christmas. Await their reaction.

2. Engage in your planned dialogue with the other members of staff whose help you enlisted, which might go something like this.

   'We hope you're not going to wear those in the staffroom.'
   'Why not?'
   'They look silly.'
   'But I'm just having a bit of fun.'
   'If that's how you behave I don't think we shall want you at the Christmas dinner.'
   'I'm looking forward to the Christmas dinner.'
   'Well, we're not looking forward to everyone looking at us because of your silly antlers.'
   'I can't help it. I just enjoy being a bit different.'
   'Go and be different somewhere else then.'
   'But isn't Christmas a time for joining in parties and having fun?'
   'Not with you, antler man/woman!'

3. Assure the children that you're just having some fun, but invite them to think seriously about the role play. What attitudes concerned them? How does it feel to be 'picked on' and excluded from fun and friendships?

4. Lighten the mood by introducing the song 'Rudolph the red-nosed reindeer'. Review the story of the song together with the children (it could be translated into a fun play or dance). Emphasize the point that the different thing about Rudolph, which made him the 'odd one out', was just what was needed to make Christmas complete!

5. Sing the song together, introducing the actions. At the word 'Rudolph' or 'reindeer', put your hands either side of your head, fingers outstretched, so they look like antlers. At the word 'nose' or 'nosed', trace a circle with your index finger in front of your nose.

6. Reflect that Christmas can be great fun, but not for anyone who feels left out or alone. Invite the children to remember the first Christmas story. How did Mary and Joseph feel when they were turned away by innkeepers who said, 'Go away. We can see you're having a baby, but we've got no room.'

Remind everyone that the shepherds who came to Bethlehem were some of the poorest people, people whom others avoided.

7. Conclude by noting that, for Christians, an important word in the Christmas story is 'good will'. It's found in another song – that of the angels, who sang, 'Glory to God in the highest, and on earth peace, good will toward men!' (Luke 2.14, NKJV). 'Good will' means that God wants no one to be unhappy and left out. At Christmas, we can share fun and friendship and show the meaning of good will to others.

 Time for reflection

Play part of the song again and ask everyone to think about the words in a new way. It's not just a fun Christmas song but also about including everyone.

Prayer

Lord God,
Help us to share peace and good will,
this Christmas,
and throughout the coming year.
Amen.

 Song

'Christmas time is here' (*Come and Praise*, 127)

THE FIRST CHRISTMAS ROBIN
Christmas

Suitable for Whole School

Aim

To retell a Christmas legend to highlight the importance of practical help.

Preparation and materials

- Find an image of a Christmas robin and have the means available to display it during the assembly (check copyright).
- You could wear some red clothing, but this is optional.
- You can simply read the story or it could be presented by a group of children.
- **Note:** It is important to point out to the children that they should *never* light fires, especially not in a stable.
- Either have available the song 'When the red red robin comes bob bob bobbin' along' and the means to play it to sing along to or choose one of the other options given in the 'Songs' section, below.

Assembly

1. Introduce the theme by asking if anyone has received or sent a Christmas card with a robin on it. Refer to the cards and decorations we have at Christmas and comment that robins make a bright and cheerful contribution to our Christmas celebrations.

2. Explain that robins first found their way on to Christmas cards because Victorian postmen wore bright red uniforms and were nicknamed 'robins'. Instead of showing postmen delivering the Christmas mail, card designers showed robins carrying envelopes in their beaks and with bags of letters around their necks!

3. Mention, too, that other Christmas legends tell how the robin got such beautiful red feathers and you are now going to tell them one of these, called 'The first Christmas robin'.

The first Christmas robin

When Mary and Joseph went to Bethlehem, there was nowhere for them to stay, so Jesus was born in a stable.

Stables are cold and draughty places, so Joseph carefully lit a small fire to keep Mary and her baby warm. Jesus slept safely in the manger, warmed by the fire, but, as the night grew darker and darker, the stable became colder and colder and the flames of the fire flickered lower and lower. Soon, all that was left of the fire was a dull glow.

Perhaps the little brown bird was cold or maybe it understood what was happening and wanted to help. Mary heard it flutter down on to the floor. Settling close to the ashes, the little brown bird flapped its wings to fan the embers.

Suddenly, the fire burst back into life. Mary smiled, but then, to her sorrow, she saw that the heat of the flames had singed the brown feathers on the little bird's chest and they had turned bright red. 'Thank you, little bird,' she said. 'May God forever bless you!'

So, as a reward for its kindness, the robin has kept its beautiful red feathers and it still brings warmth and cheerfulness to many people at Christmastime!

4. Reflect that this legend celebrates the importance of helping others at Christmas. Invite the children to suggest ways in which they share cheerfulness with others, such as visiting older family members, singing carols at a local shopping centre, performing in a Christmas play, helping to tidy and decorate their homes, delivering Christmas cards to friends, supporting the work of a charity . . . Helpfulness and kindness can brighten the season – just like the robin!

 Time for reflection

Be thankful for someone who has helped you this week.

How might you cheer someone up today?

Prayer
Lord God,
Thank you for bright winter robins, warmth and cheerfulness.
Amen.

 Songs

'When the red red robin comes bob bob bobbin' along'

'Christmas time is here' (*Come and Praise*, 127)

'Merry Christmas everyone' (*Songs for Every Season*, Out of the Ark Music, 1997)

THE NIGHT BEFORE CHRISTMAS
Christmas Eve

Suitable for Whole School

 Aim

To explain the significance of Christmas Eve by means of reference to the carol 'Silent night'.

 Preparation and materials

- You will need the lyrics of the carol 'Silent night' (these can be found in hymnbooks and on the Internet) printed or displayed during the assembly. You could prepare the carol in several different languages, too, as it was originally written in German. If possible, arrange for someone to play a simple guitar accompaniment to 'Silent night' in the 'Time for reflection' section of the assembly.
- Find out where and when Christmas services are being held locally to mention in the 'Assembly', Step 1, below.
- Note that, in the 'Assembly', Step 4 – about the ceasefire on Christmas Eve during the First World War – is optional.

 Assembly

1. Introduce the theme by explaining that Christmas Eve (the night before Christmas) is one of the most holy (special) nights of the year to Christians. It's the time when everyone prepares to celebrate Jesus' birth – final touches are made to decorations, festive food is bought and prepared and visitors made welcome. Churches hold services late at night so that, when midnight comes, everyone can wish one another 'Happy Christmas'. Mention some of these services being held in your community. Reflect that, therefore, Christmas is a very busy time for Christian priests and ministers – not forgetting choirs and organists, who often prepare special music for the celebrations.

2. Tell the following story in your own words.

   The story of 'Silent night'

   Almost 200 years ago, in 1818, a young Austrian priest called Father Joseph Mohr was preparing to celebrate Christmas with the congregation of his church. He knew that the church would be packed with people and everyone was looking forward to the special time that they would share together. Father Joseph, however, was sad – the church organ was broken and it couldn't be repaired in time for Christmas. It seemed that mice had eaten some of the leather parts. Father Joseph knew that everyone would be disappointed not to hear the organ play, but what could he do?

   It was Christmas Eve and Father Joseph was thinking how still and silent the church would seem without music. 'Still and silent' – the words kept coming into Father Joseph's mind. Then he remembered a Christmas poem that he had written a few years earlier.

   Father Joseph knew there was no time to waste. Taking the words of the poem from his study, he quickly put on his heavy overcoat, hat and gloves and strode out into the crisp, cold morning air. Before long he was at the house of his friend and musician Franz Gruber who welcomed him inside. Father Joseph took the poem from his pocket and handed it to his friend. 'Can you help?' he asked, 'The church organ is broken. Could you play your guitar and could you put these words to music, so that we can sing them together?'

Franz Gruber smiled. He read through the words, picked up his guitar and began to hum a tune. The notes faltered. Franz Gruber stopped, shook his head and tried again. Father Joseph listened as the words of his poem were gradually woven with the notes of the guitar into a simple but beautiful song. Soon both he and his friend were singing together:

Stille Nacht, heilige Nacht! (Silent night, holy night!)

After darkness fell, Father Joseph and Franz Gruber met again as everyone gathered for the first mass of Christmas. Families sat squeezed into the pews of the small church. No one was left out. Together, everyone listened to the story of how Mary and Joseph travelled to Bethlehem and of how Mary's baby was born in a stable because there was no room at the inn. As they heard about the shepherds and the angels' message, the small church grew still and silent.

Then, in the flickering candlelight, the new Christmas song was heard.

Accompanied quietly on the guitar, the soft, deep, voices of Father Joseph and Franz Gruber blended together with those of the choir. The melody was gentle, like a lullaby, but with beautiful echoes like angels singing.

The last notes faded away and those who were listening felt a deep sense of peace and wonder. The music had helped to make the Christmas story real. It was a really special, holy night – one that everyone remembered for a long, long time.

After Christmas, the organ was mended. The people were glad, but they were also glad that, on the night before Christmas, they had been the first to hear the carol 'Silent night'.

3. Explain that so many people liked the carol, it was eventually published (printed) and translated into other languages, so that people and choirs in churches all around the world can enjoy singing the words.

4. If including, mention that, in 1914, almost 100 years after it was written, soldiers fighting one another in the First World War sang the song and other carols together on Christmas Eve and Christmas Day in French, German and English. It led to a short time of peace. Enemies stopped fighting, greeted one another and even played football together in what became known as 'The Christmas truce'.

5. Reflect that 'Silent night' is a carol which speaks of the importance of silence and stillness. After all the busy preparations for Christmas, Christians believe that it is important on Christmas Eve to listen quietly to the story of Jesus' birth – just as the shepherds heard God's message in the silence out on the hills.

 Time for reflection

Spend a few moments in quiet, then sing 'Silent night', with guitar accompaniment, if this is possible.

 Song

'Silent night, holy night' (*Hymns Old and New* (Kevin Mayhew), 658, 2008 edition)

A GREAT DAY MADE EVEN BETTER
Epiphany (6 January)

Suitable for Whole School

 Aim

To consider how we can help to solve a problem – with reference to the story of Jesus at the Wedding in Cana (see John 2).

 Preparation and materials

- Find some appropriate wedding photographs and have the means available to display them during the assembly.
- To add drama to the storytelling, you could use a jug of water, a large opaque container, such as a mixing bowl or casserole pot, an empty wine glass and a ladle with two or three drops of red food colouring out of sight in it. When a little water is collected in the ladle and poured into the glass, it will appear to have turned into wine.

 Assembly

1. Introduce the theme of the assembly, which concerns helping one another to solve a problem and will include the story of a wedding.

2. Display some of the wedding images you prepared and explain that a wedding celebrates the love of two people who are traditionally known as the bride and groom. Their friends and family gather to support them and share in their happiness. Everyone enjoys special food and drink at a wedding reception.

3. Observe that, occasionally, things can go wrong at a wedding. A car can break down, a ring be lost or even a cake collapse. Then it's important for everyone to help one another solve the problem so the special day is not ruined.

4. Tell the Bible story of the wedding at Cana. It describes how Jesus helped to solve a problem.

   ### The wedding at Cana

   The wedding had been a great success! Everyone was happy, especially the bride and groom.

   Everyone was there – family, friends, neighbours . . . and Jesus, with his mother, Mary.

   Everyone enjoyed the delicious food and drink.

   'More to eat?' asked the bride's mother.
   'Yes please!' said the guests.
   'More to drink?' asked the bride's father.
   'Yes please!' everyone replied – which is how the problem arose.
   'There is no more drink,' whispered one of the servants. 'It's all gone.'

   How awful! How embarrassing! People held out their empty glasses, but there was no more wine. The bride's family felt very upset and ashamed. They worried that their daughter's special day would be remembered as the time when something went wrong.

'Do something!' whispered Mary to Jesus.

'It's not the right moment', he replied. 'Everybody will say I'm a show-off.'

'You must do something', insisted Mary. 'Do whatever he tells you', she told the servants.

In the corner of the room were some pots of water for washing the guests' hands.

'Fill those with fresh water,' Jesus instructed the servants.

If using the props, pour the water in the jug into the opaque container and dip your fingers into it to demonstrate that the water is clear, normal water.

'Now serve that to drink,' Jesus told the servants. They were puzzled, but did what he said.

Using the ladle containing the food colouring, gently collect some water in it and pour the 'wine' into the wine glass.

To their amazement, the water turned into lovely wine! Indeed, it was the best that anyone had ever tasted.

'More to eat?' asked the bride's mother.

'Yes please!' said the guests.

'More to drink?' asked the bride's father.

'Yes please!' everyone replied happily!

Jesus had helped to solve a problem. He had turned water into wine – and frowns into smiles. He had made a great day even better!

5. Invite everyone to consider how *they* might help to solve a problem. How would they respond if:

   – someone couldn't find their coat before playtime
   – a friend or grown-up said, 'I need some help'
   – all the pencils needed to be sharpened.

Observe that helping to solve a problem isn't showing off. It involves noticing how others are feeling and showing concern. Helping to solve a problem can make *any* day better and happier for everyone!

 Time for reflection

Prayer

Lord Jesus,
At moments when things go wrong, make us more willing and ready to help.
Help us to turn today into a better day for everyone.
Amen.

 Songs

'Give me oil in my lamp' (*Come and Praise*, 43)

'Wake up!' (*Songs for Every Assembly*, Out of the Ark Music, 1999)

FOLLOW THAT STAR!
New Year and Epiphany

Suitable for Key Stage 2

 Aim

To affirm positive values with reference to the story of the wise men.

 Preparation and materials

- Find a Christmas card image of the journey of the wise men and have the means to display it during the assembly.
- Also, prepare the following acrostic poem to display:

Support one another.
Try and try again.
Aim high.
Realize your goals.

 Assembly

1. Open by mentioning that this is the start of a New Year and the beginning of a new term. What will be learned? Where might new discoveries lead?

   Display the image of the wise men.

2. Reflect that new beginnings might be compared to setting out on a journey, then tell the story of the wise men imaginatively along the following lines.

   ### The story of the wise men

   Long ago, in a distant land, a bright star appeared.

   Some wise men saw the star and knew it marked an exciting beginning. It was a sign. A new king had been born. They set out on a long journey to find him.

   The star pointed the way and it led them to Jerusalem. 'Where's the newborn king?' asked the wise men. King Herod, who ruled Jerusalem, became very jealous and upset. His advisers also told him, 'A king will be born in Bethlehem.'

   Herod sent the wise men on their way, but asked them, 'When you find the new king, let me know – I'd like to see him, too.'

   The star still shone. It guided the wise men to the place where Mary and Joseph were staying with their baby, Jesus. The wise men joyfully knelt down and presented him with precious gifts of gold, frankincense and myrrh.

   Then they set off on their journey home, by a different route. God had warned them in a dream not to trust King Herod!

3. Suggest that the story might help us all to approach the new term wisely and well.

   Display the acrostic poem.

   Using the letters and meanings of the acrostic poem, reflect how the wise men:

   Supported one another – they shared a journey together
   Tried and tried again – they made mistakes but didn't give up
   Aimed high – they wanted to do and give their best
   Realized their goals – their long journey was rewarded.

4. Conclude with the thought that, at the start of a new term, we should keep *this* star in view.

 Time for reflection

How might you be able to help and support one another today?

How will you keep trying and not give up?

How will you give of your best . . . and find joy in success?

How will you follow your star?

> *Prayer*
> Lord God,
> Help us to:
> use every opportunity wisely
> treat other people respectfully
> overcome challenges successfully
> and live life joyfully,
> today and every day.
> **Amen.**

 Songs

'One more step along the world I go' (*Come and Praise*, 47)

'The wise may bring their learning' (*Come and Praise*, 64)

'Today' (*Songs for Every Assembly*, Out of the Ark Music, 1999)

THE WICKED KING, A SPIDER AND A NARROW ESCAPE
Epiphany (6 January)

Suitable for Whole School

Aim

To tell the story of the escape to Egypt and become more aware of the plight of refugees.

Preparation and materials

- You will need:
  - an easel
  - large sheet (A1 size) of black paper
  - glue stick
  - some white sugar or glitter in a sugar shaker or jam jar with a perforated lid
  - old sheet, to lay on the floor under the easel
  - a picture of refugees, reflecting a recent news item.

Assembly

1. Explain that 'Twelfth Night' marks the end of Christmas. Enquire if everyone has taken their Christmas trees and decorations down. Were any spiders found? (The significance of this question will become apparent later.)

2. Introduce the story of what happened after the *first* Christmas. Mary and Joseph's hopes of a safe journey home were dashed. The problem was 'wicked King Herod'. Invite involvement in the story, asking the children to follow the pantomime tradition of booing the villain and cheering the heroes. Tell them that you will help them to know when to do this by giving a thumbs up or a thumbs down sign (the first two instances in the story below are isolated to give you an idea, but continue in this vein to the end).

   Mary and Joseph flee to Egypt

   Now wicked King Herod

   (thumbs down, boo!)

   was very nasty . . . and wicked King Herod

   (thumbs down, boo!)

   was very angry. In fact, wicked King Herod *(thumbs down, boo!)* was boiling with rage, because the last of the visitors to the stable, the wise men *(thumbs up, hurray!)*, had been wise enough to *not* tell wicked King Herod *(thumbs down, boo!)* exactly where Jesus was! Well done, wise men! *(Thumbs up, hurray!)*

   Wicked King Herod *(thumbs down, boo!)* wanted to find Jesus not to worship him, but to kill him.

   'No one's more important than me,' shouted wicked King Herod. *(Thumbs down, boo!)* 'There's room for only one king in this land and that's me!'

   The King called his bodyguards and soldiers and told them to search every house in Bethlehem. They were to look for a tiny baby boy. Jesus was in great danger.

Thanks to an angel, Mary and Joseph knew that they had to escape quickly. As the soldiers knocked on doors, they quietly slipped away. They couldn't go home to Nazareth – soldiers were guarding the road. So they had to head towards Egypt.

Perhaps the spider *(thumbs up, hurray!)* travelled with them from the stable – hidden in their small bundle of belongings – or maybe the cave where Mary and Joseph found shelter was its home. Whatever the case, while the family was sleeping, the spider *(thumbs up, hurray!)* came out of its hiding place. It climbed to the roof of the entrance to the cave, dropped to the ground and began to spin a web.

Putting the sheet of black paper on the easel, use the glue stick to trace the pattern of a spider's web on to the paper.

No one could see the web. It was quite invisible, until dawn came and the cold frost formed.

Hold the sheet of paper horizontally and lightly sprinkle the sugar or glitter over the glue lines. It will stick to the glue pattern. Tip off the excess, then return the paper to the easel so the children can see.

The spider's web glistened and glittered across the mouth of the cave.

'Where are they, then?' shouted an angry voice. *(Thumbs down, boo!)*

Mary and Joseph were woken by the sound of the soldiers' voices. They shrank back into the shadows.

'You'd better look in that cave,' said one of the soldiers.

Mary and Joseph hid as best they could. The footsteps came nearer. They hardly dared to breathe! Then the footsteps stopped.

'Look at this spider's web. No one's been in there,' said another soldier.

So it was that the soldiers of wicked King Herod *(thumbs down, boo!)* went away. Mary, Joseph and the baby Jesus were safe. *(Thumbs up, hurray!)*

3. Reflect that the next time the children see a glistening spider's web, or even a spider, they may like to remember this story. They may also want to think of people across the world today who are refugees. 'Refugees' are people forced to leave their homes because they are frightened of being killed by their enemies or who perhaps have been affected by drought or famine. They are families who need refuge, safety and shelter.

Display the image of refugees.

4. Outline the background to the plight of the people in the image. Note that, often, caring organizations set up camps to assist refugees. Food and simple shelters are provided. While families are together with others they are in less danger, but, of course, they hope that one day they will be able to return home.

5. Conclude by asking the children if Mary and Joseph were ever able to go home from Egypt. You can let them know that, happily, they were able to return to Nazareth, but only after King Herod died as only then were they safe.

What happened to the spider? The story doesn't tell, but, as everyone knows, spiders are very good at finding homes to live in!

Time for reflection

> *Prayer*
>
> God of all people,
> We pray today for families who are escaping from danger –
> those who are refugees
> and those who help and protect them.
> **Amen.**

 Song

'When I needed a neighbour' (*Come and Praise*, 65)

A CHANGED PERSON
Conversion of St Paul (25 January)

Suitable for Key Stage 2

Aim

To celebrate and reflect on the story of the conversion of Paul.

Preparation and materials

- Find an image of St Paul's Cathedral, London, and have the means to display it during the assembly (optional).
- A pair of dark sunglasses could be used to symbolize Paul's experience of lost and regained sight (optional).
- Familiarize yourself with the story of Paul, given in the 'Assembly', Step 2, below, and either prepare to play the role yourself or enlist the help of a colleague to do so.
- Have available the song 'Amazing grace' and the means to play it at the end of the assembly or the lyrics to sing it. It has been chosen as it was written by John Newton to celebrate his own conversion.

Assembly

1. If using, display the image of St Paul's Cathedral, without naming it, and invite the children to identify it.

   Explain that many Christian churches are named after saints. A 'saint' is someone whose example inspires and helps others. Paul was a church leader who wrote many of the letters in the New Testament. He travelled widely to share the Christian message. He wasn't always known by the name of Paul, though – nor was he always thought of as a saint!

2. Invite everyone to listen to Paul tell his own story. If you are playing the part of Paul, turn your back to the audience for a few moments, then turn round, having assumed the role. Otherwise, hand over to the colleague who is to play him.

   Monologue: 'My name's Paul'

   Hello! My name's Paul. I used to be called Saul.

   Believe me, I wasn't a nice person! I hated anyone who believed in Jesus. I wasn't a kind person. I even stood by when his followers were killed.

   I was an angry person. I found out where the Jesus people lived and dragged them off to prison. 'That'll teach them,' I thought, 'they should behave like everyone else.' Other people agreed – 'They deserve it,' they said. 'They think they're better than us.'

   Eventually all the followers of Jesus were terrified.

   I set off to do the same in Damascus. It was a hot day and I felt hot and angry inside – very angry! Perhaps that's what caused the blinding light.

   Suddenly, I couldn't see anything. I felt dizzy. I fell to the ground.

   Put sunglasses on, if using.

   A voice spoke to me.

   'Saul . . . Saul, why are you doing this to me?'

'Who is it?' I cried out.

'It's Jesus,' said the voice. 'Why do you hate me?'

I still couldn't see.

My friends took my hand and helped me along the road. I felt helpless and, I'll admit it now, terrified. I realized that this was how I'd made other people feel. So I prayed and, although I didn't deserve it, the God of Jesus heard my prayer. He sent help.

A man called Ananias came to pray with me. He was one of the Jesus people I'd set out to kill.

'Brother Saul,' he said, 'the Lord has sent me.'

Ananias was so kind – and so forgiving.

Then my eyes were opened! I could see!

Take the sunglasses off.

What I'd done was awful, but I knew that God could change even someone as bad as me! I became a follower of Jesus, too – and now I want to tell everyone that good news!

So call me Paul – all my new friends do. It's my Christian name – a different name. The name tells how much I've changed.

3. Invite the children to respond to the story. In what ways did Saul change? Establish that:
   - he was an enemy, but became a friend
   - he was cruel, but learned kindness
   - he was uncaring, but understood his actions affected others
   - he didn't consider the views of others, but grew in understanding
   - he learned respect for God and others.

   Saul's change of name reflected his change of character. Explain that Christians describe such a change as a 'conversion'.

4. Conclude by reflecting that, today, many people across the globe continue to face hatred and violence because of their beliefs. The story of Saul challenges aggression shown towards the customs, faiths and traditions of others.

 Time for reflection

Ask the children to think about their personal attitudes and behaviour and if there are any that they need to change.

> *Prayer*
> *The world peace prayer*
> Lead me from death to life,
> from falsehood to truth.
> Lead me from despair to hope,
> from fear to trust.
> Lead me from hate to love,
> from war to peace.
> Let peace fill our heart,
> our world, our universe.

 Song

'Amazing grace' (*Hymns Old and New* (Kevin Mayhew), 34, 2008 edition)

YOUNG AND OLD TOGETHER
Candlemas (2 February)

Suitable for Whole School

Aim

To affirm the importance of encouraging and inspiring one another.

Preparation and materials

- You will need two candles – one new 25–30 cm (10–12 inches), the other an old one that has burned to a short stump, almost finished.
- Also suitable and safe candleholders for the candles, and taper or candle lighter.

Assembly

1. Begin by explaining that, in the Christian calendar, 2 February is known as Candlemas. It's a time to give thanks for light, hope and the approach of spring. In the past, ceremonies were held to bless candles for use in church.

2. Show the children the two candles. Ask, 'Which one is old? Which is new?' Observe that the short candle is old. It has burned for hours and given most of its light. Soon its flame will die and a new light will be needed.

3. Invite the children to imagine what it feels like to grow old. They may consider it 'scary' and 'sad' or a matter of 'achievement' and 'pride'. A conversation may reflect on experiences of loss and bereavement as well as the active and caring lifestyles that many older people enjoy. As they grow old, some people regret that time has passed quickly and their energies are diminished – like the old candle. Others may be glad that they can still give help and light to those around them.

4. Explain that, at Candlemas, Christians tell a story about an old man and a new baby.

The presentation of Christ in the temple

The old man was called Simeon. He was gentle and patient. Simeon often thought about the past. He remembered God's promise to help his people. Many years had passed. There was little sign that God would keep his promise, yet Simeon's faith and hope kept burning.

Light the small candle.

Simeon often went to the temple to say his prayers, but now he was growing old and tired. Sometimes he asked himself, 'What's the use?' Would God *ever* answer his prayers?

One day, although he was very tired, Simeon felt that he *must* go to the temple. It was the day that Mary and Joseph went to the temple, too. They took their new baby, Jesus, to ask God to bless him. They wanted to say thank you for his safe birth and a new beginning.

Simeon welcomed Mary and Joseph. Mary explained why they had come: 'We want God to bless our baby. His name's Jesus. Would you like to hold him?' Simeon cradled Jesus in his arms.

Lightly cradle the new candle with your hands – pausing to reflect that it's always a special moment, holding a new baby. Some will remember holding a new baby brother or sister.

It was an even more special moment for Simeon. 'After all these years,' he exclaimed, 'God has kept his promise. I've seen it with my own eyes. Now I feel at peace. Your child,' he said to Mary, 'will be a light for all the world to see.'

Light the new candle.

Simeon was overjoyed. He had experienced something exciting and new. That day was one he would remember until the end of his life, when the light of faith would still be shining.

Place both candles together in a central position.

5. Conclude by saying, 'So, at Candlemas we can be thankful for the light – the light of humanity and the light of God – that we see in one another . . . both old and young together.'

 Time for reflection

Ask the children to quietly recall a time when the patience of an older person meant much.

Invite everyone to think how older people can be encouraged and comforted by the energy and enthusiasm of the young.

Reflect that, together, like the two different candles, we can increase the light of faith in the world and keep it burning.

Prayer

Lord God,
Thank you that often the answers to our prayers are found in the company of one another, young and old together.
Amen.

 Songs

'Give me oil in my lamp' (*Come and Praise*, 43)

'Together' (*Songs for Every Assembly*, Out of the Ark Music, 1999)

SPRING

SOMETHING GOOD
Shrove Tuesday and Lent

Suitable for Whole School

 Aim

To reflect on positive choices with reference to Shrove Tuesday and the season of Lent.

 Preparation and materials

- You will need:
  - pancake
  - tube of toothpaste and an ice-cream container
  - an onion and an orange
  - bottle of vinegar and bottle of golden syrup

  kept hidden during the assembly until you need them in the 'Assembly', Step 3, below.

 Assembly

1. Start by mentioning that it is the beginning of Lent. During this season, Christians try to follow Jesus' example and aim to take positive steps to make the world a better place for everyone.

2. Explain that pancakes are made on the day before Lent begins, which is called Shrove Tuesday. Say how you make them, miming mixing the batter and pouring it into a pan before frying and flipping each pancake. The pancakes can then be topped or filled.

3. Ask the children, 'What filling would you choose?'

   Produce the pancake and have fun suggesting some alternative fillings.

   How about using toothpaste to make a lovely minty pancake? No! That would spoil it! Ice-cream would be more enjoyable.

   For a stronger flavour we could use raw onion, but that would make someone cry! Instead, an orange would be good.

   We could add vinegar, but that is so sour! Wouldn't syrup be far sweeter?

   Be prepared for some excitement and unusual suggestions! Continue in this vein for a short while, then explain that these fun choices do make a serious point. Poor decisions spoil the best of experiences, while good choices can add to the enjoyment.

4. Observe that a pancake is round, like the world. Referring to the toothpaste, onion and vinegar in turn, reflect that it's possible to spoil our environment, upset others and make choices that turn life sour.

   Invite everyone to consider how the life of a school community can be spoiled because of inconsiderate words and thoughtless actions.

5. Refer to the ice-cream, orange and syrup. Stress the importance of appropriate choices. Positive words and actions can make any school a happier and more enjoyable place to be. Invite everyone to consider what this might mean.
   Affirm the values of courtesy, kindness and fairness.

6. Return to the pancake. How will the children *fill* their day? Will everyone remember the importance of courtesy, kindness and fairness? Will they aim to make the best of every opportunity to create and achieve something good?

 Time for reflection

Let's be thankful for the fun of making pancakes and the enjoyment of eating them!

Let's be sorry for the times when fun and enjoyment have been spoiled.

This Lent, let's make positive choices that fill our world with happiness.

 Songs

'Make me a channel of your peace' (*Come and Praise*, 147)

'Song of blessing' (*Songs for Every Assembly*, Out of the Ark Music, 1999)

SORRY PANCAKES
Shrove Tuesday

Suitable for Whole School

 Aim

To mark the beginning of Lent by appreciating the importance of saying 'Sorry'.

 Preparation and materials

- You will need:
  - a frying pan and pancake ingredients – flour, eggs, milk and a little salt
  - five pancake-sized circles of yellow paper, each having one letter of the word 'sorry' clearly marked in the centre, and a marker pen
  - some extra blank yellow paper pancakes may be useful.

 Assembly

1. Mention that it is or is soon to be Pancake Day, also known as Shrove Tuesday. Briefly describe how pancakes are made by first mixing the ingredients to form a batter. Show the children the flour, eggs, milk and salt as you mention them. Mime the process of pouring the batter into the pan, frying and the excitement of flipping a pancake.

2. Reflect that pancakes are one of the easiest foods to make, but they bring to mind a word that can be very hard to say.

   Tell the children that you are going to give them some 'pancake clues'. Challenge them to decipher the word that can be very hard to say from the initial letters of the answers to the clues. As you proceed, invite five children to hold up the pancake circles to help them spell the answer – 'sorry'.
   - I'm the first letter of something white and sweet that you might sprinkle on your pancake. 'S' for sugar.
   - I'm the first letter of a large round fruit; its juice is sometimes poured on to pancakes. My name is also my colour. 'O' for orange.
   - I'm the first letter in a word describing the shape of a pancake. Flat and . . . 'R' for round.
   - I'm the first letter of the way that pancakes are often served. 'R' for rolled.
   - I'm the first letter of a word that means 'really delicious'. 'Y' for yummy!

3. Explain that pancakes are eaten as part of Christian traditions that mark the importance of saying sorry. Pancake Day, or Shrove Tuesday, is one when we prepare for a new start. In the weeks before Easter – known as Lent – Christians express sorrow for selfish and hurtful behaviour.

4. Invite the children to identify some occasions when it is appropriate to say sorry. Flip the paper 'sorry pancakes' and record the children's responses on the blank sides. Older children might be asked to reflect on world events that cause sadness and sorrow.

   Reflect that sorry can be one of the hardest words to say, but, like flipping a pancake, we have to be ready to try! Saying 'sorry' (show the letter sides of the 'sorry pancakes' again to show the word 'sorry') can help us make a new start.

Time for reflection

Review the responses written on the pancakes, which might include arguments, accidents, mistakes, misunderstandings, thoughtless words, hurt, tears.

> *Prayer*
>
> arguments . . . accidents
> mistakes . . . misunderstandings
> thoughtless words . . . hurt . . . tears
>
> Forgiving God,
> help us to say 'Sorry'.
> **Amen.**

 Song

'Pancakes' (*Songs for Every Season*, Out of the Ark Music, 1997)

GOOD ADVICE
Lent

Suitable for Key Stage 2

Aim

To recall the importance of good advice.

Preparation and materials

- Familiarize yourself with the story from Matthew 4.1–11 in the 'Assembly', Step 3, below, so that you can add some drama and read it in a flowing and imaginative way.

Assembly

1. Observe that anyone who has played in a football or netball team or, perhaps, has taken a dance or music examination will know the importance of good advice. Invite responses to this and, in conversation with the children, establish the nature of the advice given to them in such circumstances.

2. Reflect that good advice:
   - helps us to achieve our best
   - can prevent us from making mistakes
   - supports us in reaching our goals.

   Explain that, during Lent – a period of prayer and reflection before Easter – Christians focus on their goals and remember the importance of good advice.

3. A story is told about a testing time faced by Jesus. He found it helped him to remember sayings and good advice. Tell the following simple adaptation of Matthew 4.1–11 in an imaginative way with a sense of drama. Convey how Jesus was alone in the wilderness. He thought, he prayed and he fasted (ate very little) because he wanted to think about the needs of others.

   The temptation of Jesus

   Jesus was alone. He became very hungry, so hungry that he wanted to tell stones to turn into loaves of bread, but then he remembered a saying: 'Don't just give orders. Take time to listen!'

   Jesus stayed alone, listening in the wilderness. No one was around. He imagined standing high on a temple. 'Lots of people would look up to me,' thought Jesus. 'They'd see how important I am. I might even fly!' Then, other advice came into his mind: 'Don't show off! Show respect.'

   Still all alone, Jesus wondered what it would be like to rule the whole world. Just imagine that! Anyone who ruled the world could go anywhere they wished and have anything they wanted! Jesus quickly pushed that thought away. He remembered yet more good advice: 'Don't just help yourself! Help others.'

   Jesus was alone, but now he felt ready to begin his work.

4. Invite the children to recall the advice contained within the story. Successful people:
   - take time to listen – don't just give orders
   - show respect – don't show off
   - help others – don't just think of themselves.

What other advice might be remembered as everyone prepares to begin or return to work?

5. Conclude with the thought that, acting on positive advice, the school community will achieve its best.

 Time for reflection

Ask everyone to quietly consider one piece of helpful advice that they have heard. Invite them to remember and act on it.

> *Prayer*
> Lord God,
> Whatever tests and challenges we face,
> help us to remember good advice
> and be guided by it.
> **Amen.**

 Songs

'Living and learning' (*Songs for Every Assembly*, Out of the Ark Music, 1999)

'Give it all you've got' (*Songs for Every Assembly*, Out of the Ark Music, 1999)

A KING CALLED JESUS
Palm Sunday

Suitable for Whole School

Aim

To reflect on the significance of Palm Sunday.

Preparation and materials

- Gather images of beach donkeys, plus a donkey appropriate as an illustration for the story in the 'Assembly', Step 3, below, and a Palm Sunday procession and have the means to show them during the assembly (check copyright).

Assembly

1. Ask if any of the children have ridden a donkey. How did it feel? How might it have felt to the donkey?

   Show the images of beach donkeys.

   Explain that beach donkeys enjoy a well-earned rest through the winter months. Like many other animals, donkeys don't like a lot of fuss and noise. Sometimes they can be quite stubborn (not want to do what you want them to do) and that makes the story of Palm Sunday even more extraordinary.

2. Go on to explain that Palm Sunday is the Sunday before Easter. It is called this because palm leaves were waved at and strewn before Jesus as he rode into Jerusalem. It celebrates how the last week of Jesus' life began. Then, as in many parts of the world today, donkeys were used to help carry loads, even people.

3. Tell the following story in your own words.

   Show the image of a donkey selected to illustrate the story.

   Dinky the donkey

   Dinky was a young donkey. He still lived at the house where he was born. It was just outside Jerusalem, near to a place called the Mount of Olives.

   He was still being 'broken in', meaning that he was not yet fully trained or used to people.

   Imagine Dinky's surprise when, one day, two strangers came to where he was standing, outside the doorway of the house. They untied his tether to lead him away. Dinky didn't like that at all! He brayed loudly. He kicked and stamped and made such a noise that his owner rushed to the door.

   'What are you doing with my donkey?' he demanded. 'The Master needs it,' said one of the men. 'Then that's all right,' replied Dinky's owner, 'I did say that I'd help, but take good care of him.' With a few treats, Dinky was encouraged to follow the men along the road.

   A group of people sat in the shade of an ancient olive tree. 'Well done! You've got the donkey,' said a voice. 'We have,' the two men replied, 'but you'll have to be careful, he's not used to being ridden.'

   Ridden?! Dinky's ears pricked up in alarm. He stamped in annoyance. He tried to throw off the soft blanket that had been placed over his back, but then someone whispered into his ear and that seemed to make everything all right. The same person gently climbed on to his back and Dinky was led down the hill towards the town.

'It's Jesus!' called a young girl. 'Welcome, Jesus!' The man riding Dinky smiled and waved and the little donkey realized who was on his back. It was Jesus, who helped and cared for people; who told wonderful stories and taught people how to live good lives!

At the sound of his name, many others gathered round. They cheered, 'Hurray!'

Invite the children to echo these and the following words shouted by the crowd.

They called out, 'Hosanna!' They shouted, 'Praise God' and 'Welcome, Jesus'. Dinky was rather frightened by the noise, but Jesus gently patted his neck and on they went.

Some of the crowd waved palm branches like flags. They put them in the road to stop the dust flying up over Jesus. Others even laid their cloaks on the road, like a carpet, for Dinky to walk on.

'Hurray!' . . . 'Jesus is our King!' they cheered.

'A king?' thought Dinky. 'Shouldn't kings ride on great horses and in chariots – not little donkeys like me? I wouldn't hurt a thing.' Then he remembered the quiet whisper in his ear and the kind hand patting his neck and realized that neither would Jesus. In fact, Jesus had chosen to ride him – a donkey – to show that he was the king of peace.

It was a day that Dinky remembered all his life. Of course, he never really liked crowds, especially when he learned what another crowd had done to Jesus. (They had him killed – can you believe that?) Often, on a long journey or during a hard day's work, Dinky would think of the gentleness of the man he carried to Jerusalem. 'If only there were more people like Jesus,' Dinky thought, 'the world would be far more peaceful and a better place.'

4. Explain that, on Palm Sunday, Christians tell different versions of this story. Some borrow a donkey and organize processions and many carry palms and make crosses. (Display the image of a procession and refer to the cross-shaped mark on a donkey's back.) All this is undertaken to remember that Jesus was welcomed as a king of peace.

 Time for reflection

Think of all that lies ahead today and/or the Easter holidays, soon to begin. How might you show gentleness to other creatures and kindness to other people? How might you follow the way of peace?

Prayer
Lord Jesus,
We want to welcome you and shout out, 'Hosanna! Praise God!'
We want to help and serve you and share friendship and peace.

 Songs

'Hosanna!' (*Songs for Every Easter*, Out of the Ark Music, 1996)

'Sing aloud and shout hosanna!', as follows, which is based on an original Easter song, 'We have a king who rides a donkey' by Fred Kaan (Hope Publishing Company, 1968). It is sung to the tune of 'What shall we do with the drunken sailor'.

Humbly riding on a donkey
Humbly riding on a donkey
Humbly riding on a donkey
Comes a king called Jesus.

Sing aloud and shout Hosanna!
Sing aloud and shout Hosanna!
Sing aloud and shout Hosanna!
We will make him welcome.

Palm branches waving, swaying
Palm branches, waving, swaying
Palm branches waving, swaying
For a king called Jesus.

Sing aloud and shout Hosanna!

. . .

Lay out a road before him
Lay out a road before him
Lay out a road before him
For a king called Jesus.

Sing aloud and shout Hosanna!

. . .

Join hands in peace and friendship
Join hands in peace and friendship
Join hands in peace and friendship
For a king called Jesus.

Sing aloud and shout Hosanna!

. . .

A FAMILIAR VOICE
Easter

Suitable for Key Stage 2

Aim

To tell the Easter story of Jesus' appearance to Mary and reflect on the comfort found in a familiar voice.

Preparation and materials

- You will need some short recordings of a few familiar voices. These could include a well-known entertainer or members of the school community. Have the means available to play them during the assembly.
- Familiarize yourself with the story in John 20.11–18. Either read the passage from a child-friendly version of the Bible or read out the story based on it provided in the 'Assembly', Step 3, below. You could ask some children to read different parts of it.

Assembly

1. Invite everyone to listen to some of the well-known or 'familiar' voices you have gathered and identify the people who are speaking.

   Observe that voices are different and distinctive and it's often possible to recognize a person from their voice even when we can't see them.

2. Talk about the comfort and reassurance that a familiar voice can provide, especially when anyone is feeling lost or sad. Explain that this was the experience of one of Jesus' friends, Mary.

3. Either read John 20.11–18 from the Bible or the following, together with some of the children if you have chosen to do so.

   A comforting voice

   Mary cried and cried.
   Jesus had died.
   And she missed him so much.

   Mary cried and cried.
   She had gone to where Jesus was buried,
   but his body was gone.

   Mary cried and cried.
   Tears filled her eyes and ran down her cheeks.
   So she didn't see that someone else was in the garden.

   'What's wrong?' asked a voice.
   (Mary thought it was the gardener.)
   'Where's Jesus?' she sobbed.
   'What have you done with him?'

   'Mary,' the voice said gently.
   'Mary. Don't cry.'
   'Don't be upset, Mary.'

It was the voice of Jesus!
'Teacher!' Mary gasped.
She reached out towards him.
'Don't try to hold on to me,' the voice said,
'I have to go – go and tell the others.'

Mary ran from the garden to tell her friends.
Jesus was alive!
She was still crying,
but now the tears were ones of joy!

4. Remind the children about what they did at the beginning of the assembly. We recognized people by their voices. Mary recognized Jesus by his voice. Acknowledge that some might find this story strange, but many people remember (and sometimes imagine they hear) the voice of those who are dear to them. At difficult times the thought of a familiar voice can provide inspiration and guidance.

5. Conclude with the thought that Jesus called Mary by name. Whenever a familiar voice calls our name, we know that someone cares!

 Time for reflection

Think and pray quietly for a few moments.

Imagine the voice of someone you know well . . . maybe someone at home . . . or a teacher . . . or someone you remember . . .

What are they encouraging you to do today?

Focus on that goal or new beginning and find strength to achieve it from the example of Jesus and with the support of all the friends who know you by name.

What will you have to tell others when you leave school today?

 Songs

'God of the morning' (*Come and Praise*, 105)

'Celebrate' or 'The gift of life' (*Songs for Every Easter*, Out of the Ark Music, 1996)

IT'S GREAT TO BE ALIVE!
Easter

Suitable for Reception and Key Stage 1

Aim

To celebrate spring and the story of Easter.

Preparation and materials

- You will need an assortment of springtime flowers and Easter decorations.
- You will also need six A4 sheets of card, each with one of the letters of the word 'Easter' written or printed on it to tell the story in the 'Assembly', Step 2, below. This version of the Easter story is based on Matthew 28.1–9.

Assembly

1. Introduce the flowers and Easter decorations. Reflect that people have always welcomed and celebrated the arrival of spring. It's a joyful new beginning after the long cold months of winter.

   Flowers, eggs, chicks and rabbits are also associated with a festival called Easter. Easter welcomes the new life of spring. It's also the time when Christians joyfully celebrate Jesus' resurrection (his return to life), having experienced the darkness and sorrow of Good Friday.

2. *Have your cards with the letters of the word 'Easter' ready to tell the following story of the first Easter Day.*

   ### The first Easter Day

   'E' is for 'early'. Very early in the morning, Jesus' friends went to the place where his body had been buried. It was still dark and they felt very sad and afraid. They trembled as they made their way to the tomb.

   'A' is for an 'angel' who told them not to be frightened. 'Jesus is alive,' the angel said. 'Don't come to look for him here. You'll find he's with you everywhere'.

   'S' is for the large 'stone' that had been rolled back from the entrance to the tomb. Jesus' friends could see inside. It was empty and filled with light. They were completely shocked and surprised!

   'T' is for 'telling'. 'Go and tell the others,' said the angel. They hurried off to tell the other followers of Jesus who were still at home.

   'E' is for 'excitement'. Suddenly Jesus met them and said, 'Peace be with you'. It was a wonderful moment that they would always remember.

   'R' is for 'risen'. Now the sun had risen in the sky and Jesus' friends knew that Jesus had risen, too. They were filled with happiness. It was great to be alive!

Time for reflection

Invite everyone to join in a joyful thank-you verse, responding to the phrase 'It's Easter!' by agreeing: 'It's great to be alive!'

> The sun is shining and birds are singing.
> It's Easter! **It's great to be alive!**

Look at the bright flowers!
It's Easter! **It's great to be alive!**

Everything is alive and growing.
It's Easter! **It's great to be alive!**

Don't be sad. Never despair.
It's Easter! **It's great to be alive!**

Share the good news!
It's Easter! **It's great to be alive!**

 Songs

'Now spring is here' (*Songs for Every Easter*, Out of the Ark Music, 1996)

'Easter jubilation' (*Songs for Every Easter*, Out of the Ark Music, 1996)

'All in an Easter garden' (*Come and Praise*, 130)

NOT HIDDEN NOW!
Easter

Suitable for Reception and Key Stage 1

Aim

To celebrate springtime beginnings in the context of the Easter story.

Preparation and materials

- Work out and rehearse appropriate actions to support the descriptions in the 'Assembly' text, Step 2 onwards, below.

Assembly

1. Explain that you want to celebrate springtime and Easter. Tell the children that you are going to be referring to some hidden things that everyone in the school will soon see. You are going to be saying the phrase 'It's not hidden now!' and, every time you do, you want the children to exclaim, 'Wow!' Rehearse this a couple of times and then proceed along the following lines, inviting the children to imagine what springtime and Easter are like.

2. A seed is planted in the soil.

   Mime the actions of planting a seed as you continue.

   It's very small. Cover it over gently. The tiny dry seed is hidden away, but the rain waters it, the sun warms it and roots grow to hold it fast in the soil. A shoot pushes up towards the light. Leaves unfold. The plant springs up tall!

   It's not hidden now! **Wow!**

3. An egg is in a secret nest. The mother hen keeps it warm. Hidden inside, a tiny bird grows.

   Pretend to be an unhatched chick as you continue.

   It gets bigger and stronger. It moves around inside the egg. Eventually, the chick struggles to break free. Crack! The shell's broken! A fluffy yellow chick has hatched!

   It's not hidden now! **Wow!**

4. You can't see the sun because it's night-time and the world is dark.

   Close your eyes and shiver.

   Everything is shadowy and cold. Look! Now the sky is turning orange. Listen! The birds are singing! The sun is slowly rising. Its light is getting brighter. Morning has come.

   Open your eyes and stretch your arms.

   Can you feel the warmth of the golden sunshine?

   It's not hidden now! **Wow!**

5. Jesus' friends are crying.

   Wipe your cheeks as if wiping away tears.

   They are very sad. Jesus has died. No one sees them. It's still very early in the morning. They are going to the garden where Jesus was buried. The entrance to his tomb is closed with a great big stone.

Form a large circle with your arms.

The stone has been moved!

Stand with open uplifted arms.

Look! There's a shining angel! The angel says that Jesus is alive and so they mustn't be upset! No one is to be afraid!

Just like a seed growing, an egg hatching or the sun rising, it's a new beginning! Soon Jesus' friends are smiling.

All smile.

Everyone is happy! 'Come and celebrate with us,' they say. 'God's done a great thing. It's not hidden now!' **Wow!**

 Time for reflection

Introduce the slightly different response of 'Wow! It's Easter!'

Springtime has come.
It's not hidden now!
Wow! It's Easter!

New life is born.
It's not hidden now!
Wow! It's Easter!

Light is shining.
It's not hidden now!
Wow! It's Easter!

God's done a great thing.
It's not hidden now!
Wow! It's Easter!

Joy fills the world.
It's not hidden now!
Wow! It's Easter!

 Songs

Based on 'Christmas time is here' (*Come and Praise*, 127).

Eastertime is here, come and celebrate,

Come and celebrate, come and celebrate.

Eastertime is here, come and celebrate.

It is spring, spring, spring!

Seeds are growing tall . . .

Birds are building nests . . .

Wintertime is past . . .

Days are warm and bright . . .

New life's all around . . .

'It must be spring' (*It Must be Spring*, Out of the Ark Music, 2001)

'New beginnings' (*A Spring Thing*, Out of the Ark Music, 2009)

SUMMER

DOWN TO JUST TEN
Easter

Suitable for Key Stage 2

 Aim

To use the story of Jesus' appearance to his disciples in the upper room to demonstrate the value of a positive response to setbacks.

 Preparation and materials

- For the role play of a football match, you will need a microphone – real or pretend – the help of a colleague and a whistle for him or her to blow 'off-stage', plus a copy of the script in the 'Assembly', Step 1, below, for him or her to know when to blow the whistle.
- Familiarize yourself with the part of the Easter story when Jesus appears to the disciples in the upper room in John 20.19–21, which is referred to in the 'Assembly', Step 5.
- Have available the song 'When you walk through a storm' by Gerry and the Pacemakers and the means to play it at the end of the assembly (optional, but check copyright if you decide to include it). See the 'Songs' section for alternative suggestions.

 Assembly

1. Begin by enthusiastically involving everyone in the following role play, in which you commentate on a football match and the children imagine they are listening to this on the radio or watching it on television. Invite half of those present to actively support the Northern Lights and the rest to enthusiastically cheer on the Southern Stars. Be warned, know your audience – this part of the assembly may require some firm refereeing!

   The Northern Lights v. the Southern Stars

   Hello, and welcome to the Triumph Sports ground. It's this year's final of the Under-14s football tournament and the Northern Lights are locked in a keenly contested match with the Southern Stars.

   We're approaching the eightieth minute of the match and the score is Northern Lights 3,

   invite cheer

   Southern Stars 3!

   Invite cheer.

   Northern Lights have just been awarded a free kick a little way outside the centre circle.

   Whistle.

   The ball's been passed out wide . . . back again to the centre . . . that's a good pass . . .

   continue to invite support

   and the striker is making a run on goal . . . he's round the first defender . . . past the second . . . there's some skill here.

Into the box . . . he's looking at an open goal . . . but, oh, he's down!

Whistle.

Now, was that a dive or a trip from the remaining defender? The striker's still on the ground. The defender's gesturing, 'It wasn't me'. The referee's gone over to the linesman . . . He's calling the defender over . . . and it's a red card! The Southern Stars' defender has been sent off! He's making his way off the pitch.

Now the referee's pointing to the spot . . .

Whistle.

A penalty!! Let's see what happens . . .

The Northern Lights' striker places the ball on the spot . . . He steps back . . . pauses . . .

Whistle

and puts the ball into the back of the net.

Whistle.

It's Northern Lights 4, Southern Stars 3!

So, now, with just a few minutes remaining, this is a real test of character for the Southern Stars. They've lost a player, sent-off, and the realization dawns, 'We're down to ten'. How will the ten respond?

2. Pause and invite the children to reflect on all they've heard. How will the remaining ten players feel? Explore their emotions of anger, disappointment and frustration.

   - These may be directed towards their unfortunate teammate who has 'let them down'. Recognize, however, that the trip may have been simply caused by a careless or overenthusiastic tackle – a bad mistake rather than deliberate.
   - There may be frustration about the referee's decision. Without rules and referees, however, there could be no game and referees should not be subjected to protest and abuse, which is, after all, another sending off offence!
   - If it is thought that the opposing player 'dived', there will, naturally, be feelings of anger. Deliberate dives are dishonest and unsporting, but, in the absence of other evidence, we must accept the referee's view of things.
   - The remaining ten players will feel dispirited and fear that 'they have lost the match'.

3. Ask what advice the children would give to the remaining ten were they the team manager. Suggestions might include, 'Keep your heads up', 'Don't think you're beaten', 'You can still do it', 'Don't lose heart', 'Get back into the game'.

   Despite the setback, the remaining ten must maintain a positive attitude and their desire to win! The ten must be *ten*acious! That means they must hold on, keep trying and not give up.

4. Reflect that setbacks and disappointments are experienced in many different ways, not just on the football field. Sometimes it isn't easy to achieve our life goals. Keeping a positive attitude is so important whenever we face testing and difficult situations. Be *ten*acious! Don't give in!

5. Refer to the Easter story. After Jesus had been killed, there was a time when his 'team' was 'down to ten men'. Judas (who had betrayed Jesus) was no longer one of the twelve disciples and Thomas wasn't with the others as they met together behind locked doors. That left just ten disappointed and dispirited people who 'thought it was all over'.

How wrong they were! The risen Lord came to them, saying, 'Peace be with you' (John 20.21). The ten disciples were encouraged to not give in. They overcame their doubts and fears. Jesus told them that there was still much work to do. He said, 'As the Father has sent me, so I send you' (John 20.21). A really hard challenge lay ahead of them, but the ten faced it positively. There was still everything to play for!

6. Refer to the words of the song you will play shortly – 'When you walk through a storm' by Gerry and the Pacemakers: 'When you walk through a storm, hold your head up high'. Often associated with Liverpool United, it's a song that has helped many people through disappointment and disaster. Alternatively, talk about the words of the hymns suggested in the 'Songs' section below or a hymn of your choice.

 Time for reflection

Prayer
Lord Jesus,
When we feel that all is lost, help us to hold on to our dreams,
to look forward with faith and hear your words:
'Peace be with you'.
Amen.

 Songs

'When you walk through a storm' by Gerry and the Pacemakers

'Be bold, be strong', 'Fight the good fight with all thy might' (*Hymns Old and New* (Kevin Mayhew), 60 and 181, 2008 edition) or a positive Easter hymn of your choice

TRY AGAIN!
Easter

Suitable for Whole School

Aim

To tell an Easter story showing the importance of perseverance.

Preparation and materials

- Familiarize yourself with the story about fishing in the 'Assembly', Step 3, below, and the responses the children are to make, which are indicated in bold in Steps 2 and 3. It's based on John 21.1–14.
- Find an image of a fisherman casting a fishing net and have the means to display it, if possible, as this will help to introduce the assembly.

Assembly

1. Introduce the assembly by saying that you are going to tell a story about fishing. The story describes how fish can be caught by casting nets into the water. Show the image of a fisherman casting a net. Explain that this is a traditional method of catching fish that requires much patience and skill.

2. Invite the children to imagine fishing in this way. They will need to distinguish between their right-hand and left-hand sides and join in with the responses.
   - Begin by pretending to cast a net to your *left*, using the phrase, 'Ready, steady . . . **Throw!**'
   - Imagine pulling the net in, saying, 'All together! **Heave-ho!**'
   - Shake your head despondently, saying, 'We've caught . . . absolutely **nothing!**'

   Encourage everyone to join in. Observe that the task of catching fish isn't easy and there is always the temptation to give in, but successful fishermen have practised for a long time and learned from others. Practise the actions and responses.

3. Tell the story of Jesus' appearance to his followers at the lakeside, using the actions and responses you have just practised all together.

   If at first you don't succeed . . .

   Jesus' friends had spent all night fishing.
   They had cast the net out: 'Ready, steady . . . **throw!**'
   They had drawn it in again: 'All together! **Heave-ho!**'
   and they had caught . . . absolutely **nothing!**

   So they had tried again . . .
   casting the net out: 'Ready, steady . . . **throw!**'
   drawing it in again: 'All together! **Heave-ho!**'
   and they had caught . . . absolutely **nothing!**

   Again . . .
   they had cast the net out: 'Ready, steady . . . **throw!**'
   they had drawn it in again: 'All together! **Heave-ho!**'
   and they had caught . . . absolutely **nothing!**

   Their efforts seemed hopeless. They felt tired and disappointed.
   'What's the use? Let's give up,' said some.

After all, they'd spent all night . . .
casting the net out: 'Ready, steady . . . **throw!**'
drawing it in again: 'All together! **Heave-ho!**'
and they had caught . . . absolutely **nothing!**

Then someone standing on the shore called out to them:
'Try again! Try again, from the other side of the boat.'
'What difference will that make?' grumbled the fishermen.

But they tried again, this time on the *right* side,
casting the net out: 'Ready, steady . . . **throw!**'
drawing it in again: 'All together! **Heave-ho!**'
and this time they caught, '. . . together! **Heave-ho!**'
'Together again! **Heave-ho!**'
Just look at all those fish!

There were so many fish that the fishermen needed to help one another to drag the net to the shore. Peter suddenly realized that the person on the shore was Jesus! He'd lit a small fire on the beach. Jesus invited them to cook some of the fish. They ate it with bread and enjoyed a tasty breakfast together. Everyone felt satisfied.

Until Jesus had come to help, the fishermen had spent all night . . .

and they had caught . . . absolutely **nothing!**

Now, Jesus' friends felt that they could succeed at anything!

4. Invite the children to reflect on the story. Discuss how the fishermen felt. Ask, 'Have you ever struggled for a long time with a difficult task? Has anyone helped you to succeed?' Observe that, when faced with difficulties, it's important to keep trying.

5. Refer to the school day. What challenges will be faced? How might this story be a source of help and encouragement?

 Time for reflection

Today is a new day . . .

- – a day to approach challenges in a fresh way
- – a day to be open to new ideas and advice
- – a day to keep trying and carry on
- – a day to encourage and help one another.

Prayer

Lord Jesus,
When we complain, 'It won't work out', help us to remember that we can work things out together.
When we say, 'I'm tired', help us to make a fresh start.
When we insist, 'I can't', help us to see how we can succeed.
Amen.

 Songs

'The gift of life' (*Songs for Every Easter*, Out of the Ark Music, 1999)

'Believe' (Lin Marsh, Sing Up website (at <www.singup.org>) or *Singbook*, Youth Music and Faber Music, 2009)

'Lord of all hopefulness' (*Come and Praise*, 52)

SENT ON AN ERRAND
Easter/Ascension

Suitable for Whole School

 Aim

To focus on an Eastertide story and the privilege of being trusted with responsibilities.

 Preparation and materials

- Prepare a short shopping list.
- Familiarize yourself with the words of Matthew 28.16–20 and the retelling of them given in the 'Assembly', Step 4, below.
- If possible, gather some images of pupils undertaking errands and tasks in school and have the means to display them during the assembly.

 Assembly

1. Ask the children, 'Have you ever been sent on an errand?' Establish that this means 'going to do a task on behalf of someone else'. In school, it might involve being sent to take the register to the office or give a message to another teacher. At home, some of the older children have perhaps been trusted to go to a local shop or take something to a relative or neighbour. Invite the children to give other examples.

2. Ask the children, 'How does it feel to be trusted with an errand? Has anyone ever forgotten what they have been sent to do?' and discuss their answers.

3. Show and review the shopping list you made. Writing down a list like this makes sure that everything is remembered.

4. Refer to the Easter story. Christians remember how Jesus sent his followers on a rather different and important 'errand'. Retell what happened along the following lines.

   Jesus gives the disciples a message to deliver

   Jesus and his friends walked to the top of a high mountain. 'How far can you see?' Jesus asked. 'Miles and miles,' his friends replied. 'I want my message to travel a long way,' Jesus said. 'I want you to travel as far as you can and tell it to as many people as possible. Welcome and help anyone who wants to follow me.' Jesus' friends looked nervous and uncertain. 'Don't worry,' he told them. 'Wherever you are, think of me. Remember what I've told you!'

5. Invite everyone to imagine how Jesus' friends felt. Reflect how encouragement and confidence can be found in undertaking errands together with others.

6. Did Jesus' friends complete their errand? Observe that his message was indeed taken to others. Still, today, Christians continue to believe that they are sent to share a message of friendship and peace.

7. Conclude by suggesting that anyone sent on an errand might wish to remember the Easter story. Jesus trusted his friends to help. Can we be trusted to follow and carry out instructions?

Time for reflection

Be thankful for:

- being trusted to help someone
- the satisfaction of completing an errand
- the words, 'Thank you' or 'Well done'.

Prayer
Lord Jesus,
Your friends took a message of peace to others.
Thank you for trusting us to do the same.
Amen.

 Songs

'Give it all you've got' (*Songs for Every Assembly*, Out of the Ark Music, 1999)

'Go, tell it on the mountain' (*Come and Praise*, 24)

WAIT!
Ascension

Suitable for Whole School

Aim

To consider the need to wait patiently, with reference to Ascension Day.

Preparation and materials

- You will need an outline or images of traffic lights and the means to display them during the assembly.
- Reference is made to Ascension Day, the date of which varies, but it falls 40 days after Easter Sunday. The story of Jesus' ascension is found in Acts 1.1–9.

Assembly

1. Greet the children and affirm the patience of those who took their places first. Ask, 'How well can you wait? How long can you wait?'

   Refer to Ascension Day, the fortieth day after Easter. Explain that this is when Christians mark the end of Jesus' time on Earth. The Bible says that he was 'lifted up, and a cloud took him out of their sight' (Acts 1.9). The work of Jesus wasn't finished, however. He told his followers to go and tell all the world about him (Acts 1.8). He also instructed them to *wait* until they were prepared and ready. He said that God would fill them with joy and love, they just had to *wait* and see (Acts 1.4)! Stress that Jesus' friends didn't know *how long* they would have to wait (Acts 1.7).

2. Ask the children to recall and describe experiences of waiting. These might include:
   - waiting for a special day, such as a birthday or Christmas
   - waiting for a special moment, such as performing in a play or concert or queuing for a theme park ride
   - waiting for things to change, such as recovering from an illness or the rain to stop
   - waiting for a new beginning, such as sowing and growing seeds, watching for an egg to hatch or expecting the birth of a baby.

   Invite the children to describe the emotions felt while waiting. Waiting often involves a mixture of frustration and anticipation.

3. Observe that, within a school, it's often necessary to wait. Children must:
   - wait their turn to use equipment or participate in an activity
   - wait until they have listened to instructions and a teacher has finished speaking
   - wait while they consider how to approach a task.

4. Showing the outline or images of traffic lights, refer to the red, amber, green sequence and review the importance of waiting:
   - waiting can help us to *stop* and listen (red)
   - it can help prevent mistakes and accidents
   - waiting can help us to *get ready* (red and amber)
   - it can allow us to think and pray
   - waiting means that we are prepared when it's time to *go* (green light)
   - it ensures that we go in the right direction.

5. Conclude by revisiting the question, 'So, how will waiting be important for you in school today? How good are you at waiting?' Observe that sometimes, like Jesus' friends, we must wait to make the most of opportunities.

 Time for reflection

Waiting can seem endless.

    'How much longer?' we ask.
    But the waiting time
    can be a time to listen and learn.
    The waiting time
    can make us more ready
    to take our turn.

Let's remember the importance of waiting today and aim to wait patiently and well.

 Songs

'Give us hope, Lord' (*Come and Praise*, 87)

'Sometimes I wonder' (*Songs for Every Assembly*, Out of the Ark Music, 1999)

PUMP UP ONE ANOTHER!
Pentecost/Whitsun

Suitable for Whole School

Aim

To recognize the importance of encouragement.

Preparation and materials

- Save up some awards or achievement certificates to present at the beginning of this assembly.
- You will need three or four balloons and a balloon pump.
- The encouraging verses in the 'Assembly', Step 6, below, are based on Acts 2.42 and 44.
- Use either 'Pentecost' or 'Whitsun', whichever name is used most locally.

Assembly

1. Begin this assembly by presenting the awards or achievement certificates. On behalf of everyone present say, 'Well done!' Affirm the efforts of the whole school community.

2. Produce an uninflated balloon, hold it up and reflect that a little bit of encouragement can mean so much, especially when we are feeling a bit *flat*. Encouragement fills us with confidence and helps us to realize our potential, just as a balloon takes shape when it's filled with air.

   Using the pump, start to inflate the balloon.

3. Invite everyone to think of some really encouraging words and phrases as you pump. As each one is suggested, vigorously puff some air into the balloon. Phrases might include, 'That was brilliant', 'You're getting better', 'Don't worry', 'That was a good effort', 'Go on, have a go', 'Try again', 'You're a star', 'That's really special!', 'Come on, let's all work at it together', 'It isn't as hard as you think', 'You needn't be frightened', 'I'll come with you' . . .

4. When the first balloon is almost full, remark that 'It doesn't do for us to get too puffed up – perhaps there are others who need encouragement as well.'

   Tie off the first balloon and start to inflate another. Aim to blow up at least a couple of balloons.

   Ask the children to encourage you as you blow up the balloons with a 'Keep going!' Also, observe that, like the air, encouragement can sometimes be quiet and unseen, but everyone can see its effect.

5. Remind everyone that, just as positive and encouraging words bring out the best in others, negative and careless comments – such as, 'That's not very good', 'You're useless', 'How stupid!' – can make other people feel small and deflated.

   Release some air from a balloon as you say this.

   So, we need to remember how to encourage one another. We need to 'pump up one another'.

6. Explain that, at Pentecost/Whitsun, Christians celebrate the 'birthday' of the Christian Church. Inflate another balloon to highlight the importance of encouragement for the first Christians.

   The first followers of Jesus encouraged one another (Acts 2.42 and 44).

   > 'Don't be afraid,' they said.
   > They enjoyed being together.
   > 'We can be strong,' they said.
   > They taught one another the story of Jesus.
   > 'That's brilliant,' they said.
   > They helped one another.
   > 'Thank you,' they said.
   > They said their prayers every day.
   > 'Let's serve God together,' they said.

   Jesus also promised his friends that they would be filled with the Holy Spirit – the 'helper' or 'encourager' (John 15.26). Pumped up with encouragement, their belief grew and a new community of faith took shape.

 Time for reflection

Take pride in something that you've recently achieved.

Be thankful for someone who has helped you and said, 'Well done.'

How might you encourage someone else today?

> *Prayer*
> Loving God,
> Help us to encourage one another,
> to grow in confidence and discover new gifts and abilities,
> today, and every day.
> **Amen.**

 Songs

'It's a new day' (*Come and Praise*, 106, substituting the words 'To encourage one another' for the third line in each verse)

'Give it all you've got' (*Songs for Every Easter*, Out of the Ark Music, 1996)

'Well done' (*Songs for Every Assembly*, Out of the Ark Music, 1999)

THESE LEGS WERE MADE FOR WALKING
Walk to School Week (May)

Suitable for Whole School

 Aim

To reflect on the benefits and enjoyment to be gained from walking and support 'walk to school' initiatives.

 Preparation and materials

- Gather a selection of appropriate images, such as:
  - large shoeprints
  - a globe or the Earth
  - a sign showing the name of your city, town or village or a picture of the local area
  - a person exercising
  - some thought bubbles
  - a flower in a vase or an image of the beauty of nature

  and have the means to display them during the assembly (check copyright).
- Prior to the assembly, a class might like to carry out a survey of the ways in which the children travel to school and present their results in the 'Assembly', Step 1, below.
- Also prior to the assembly, the children could undertake and record an interview with one or more older members of the community about how it used to be common to walk long distances to school when they were young and read out or play these in the 'Assembly', Step 3.
- You will need four readers for the 'Time for reflection' section of the assembly.

 Assembly

1. If a class did a survey of the different ways in which the children travel to school prior to the assembly, ask them to present their results. If not, do a quick survey now. How many have caught a bus? Come by car? Ridden a bike? Walked?

2. Introduce the 'Walk to School' initiative. Walk to School Week in the UK is held in May and October is International Walk to School Month.

3. Reflect that, in rural areas in other parts of the world, there are often few ways to travel, so children walk long distances to school. Many older people in rural areas of the UK can also recall walking considerable distances to and from school in all weathers.

   If the children undertook an interview or interviews with older members of the community, they could play their recordings or read out what the interviewees said about their experiences of travelling to school when they were young.

   Suggest that while it may not be practical for everyone to walk to school, there would be real benefits if more people did.

4. *Using appropriate images, gradually build up a display to illustrate the next five points.*

   (a) Walking is good for the planet. The fuel that cars and buses burn contributes to global warming. The more footsteps we take, the smaller our 'carbon footprint' will be. Walkers are also more aware of the environment. They notice different plants and creatures and can observe the changing seasons.

(b) Walking is good for communities. Cars can make the area around a school gate dangerous and they can become a nuisance for people who live nearby. When we walk, we meet other people, say 'Hello' and get to know our neighbours. Walking can make cities, towns and villages friendlier and safer places to live.

(c) Walking is good for our bodies. Exercise helps to keep us fit and healthy. It stretches our muscles, strengthens our bones, hearts and lungs and makes us feel better.

(d) Walking is good for our minds. A walk to school is a good way to wake up and help us focus on the new day. At the end of the school day, the walk home can help us to start to relax and wind down. Walking can also exercise our brains and help us to think clearly!

(e) Walking is good for our spirits. There are times when we need to slow down to appreciate the beauty of the world around us and realize it's good to be alive! The whole of life is like a journey, to be taken one step at a time.

5. The Bible tells us how Jesus walked with his disciples. For example, the story of the two disciples on the road to Emmaus (Luke 24.13–32) tells how the risen Jesus walked with them when they were very sad and upset. It was a long and tiring journey to their village, but, after they arrived home, they had the joy of knowing that Jesus had been with them.

6. Conclude by suggesting that our legs can enable us to be 'all-terrain' people. Walking can take us to wonderful places that cars cannot reach! Has anyone enjoyed walking to places other than school? An older child or member of staff might share an enjoyment of walking. Hidden tracks, high hills and peaceful places (as well as school!) are all accessible if we remember that our legs are made for walking!

 Time for reflection

Reader 1: Dogs and cats have four.
Reader 2: Beetles have six.
Reader 3: Spiders have eight.
Reader 4: Centipedes have . . . too many to count!
All: A lot of legs!
Reader 1: We humans have just two – and learning to walk is a great achievement.
Reader 2: No longer babies, we become toddlers and can explore the world around us.
Reader 3: Along the path of life there are always new things to discover . . . by walking!
Reader 4: The first step of the journey is often the most difficult to take.
Reader 1: Dogs and cats have four.
Reader 2: Beetles have six.
Reader 3: Spiders have eight.
Reader 4: Centipedes have . . . too many to count!
Readers 1 and 2: We humans have just two . . .
All: . . . legs, that are made for walking!

(*Note: Few centipedes actually have 100 legs. In the UK, the common centipede,* Lithobius forficatus, *has a mere 30!*)

 Song

'One more step along the world I go' (*Come and Praise*, 47)

DIDN'T WE HAVE A LOVELY TIME . . .
End of the school year

Co-written with Laura Barker

Suitable for Key Stage 1

Aims

To celebrate the experience of a day at the seaside.

Preparation and materials

- In many Church calendars, the second Sunday in July is kept as Sea Sunday. Special events and outdoor services are held in seaside towns. Funds are raised for organizations, such as the Royal National Lifeboat Institution, that promote sea safety.
- Find an image of a (local) seaside town and have the means to display it during the assembly. Alternatively, a focus could be created with some beach toys, shells, sand and seaside souvenirs.
- To encourage participation in the imaginary trip to the seaside in the 'Assembly', Step 2 onwards, an opportunity might be given for the children to talk together briefly in pairs before you begin.

Assembly

1. Refer to the approaching summer holidays. They may provide the opportunity to go away on holiday or out on day trips. Ask if anyone has been to the seaside. Where did they go?

2. The seaside excites all our senses. Invite the children to accompany you on an imaginary trip to the coast. Let them talk together briefly in pairs at this point, if this option has been chosen.

3. Let's imagine we're at *(name)*. Let's go down to the beach. What can you see?

   The sun sparkling on the sea. Distant ships on the horizon. Other children building sandcastles and paddling in the water. Shells nestling in the sand. Creatures in the rock pools.

   What can you hear?

   The waves lapping and splashing on the shore. Children shouting and laughing. Music from the funfair. The cry of seagulls.

   What can you feel?

   The rough grains of sand between your toes. The warm sun. Remember to put on some sun lotion! The cold water as you paddle. The towel as you dry yourself.

   What can you smell?

   The saltiness of the sea and seaweed. Your sun lotion. Fish and chips from the beach café.

   Are you hungry? What's your favourite seaside taste?

   Fish and chips. Candyfloss. Seaside rock. Ice-cream.

   Are you feeling tired? It's been a brilliant day. What have you enjoyed the most?

4. Days at the seaside have been popular ever since railways were first built. Railways meant that people were able to travel easily to the coast. Nowadays most visitors to the seaside travel by car or coach. Many buy souvenirs to remind them of their trip *(show examples)* and keep shells or pebbles collected from the beach *(show examples)*.

5. How will you remember today's trip? Perhaps most of all for the way in which it excited all your senses!

 Time for reflection

The seaside is an exciting place with much to enjoy. Be thankful for a day trip that you remember or one that you are looking forward to.

> *Prayer*
> Creator God,
> Thank you for the many ways in which we enjoy your world –
> through sight and sound,
> touch, smell and taste.
> Thank you for the excitement of new experiences
> and different places,
> nearby and far away.
> **Amen.**

 Songs

'Lazy days' (*Songs for Every Season*, Out of the Ark Music, 1997)

'Fun at the seaside' (*Here Comes Summer*, Out of the Ark Music, 2011)

ONE STEP AT A TIME
Last week of term

Suitable for Whole School

 Aims

To celebrate achievements and affirm positive attitudes towards change.

 Preparation and materials

- You will need some blue sheeting or other cloth to represent water and sufficient paving blocks or bricks to construct a 'river' and a set of five stepping stones.
- Find an image of stepping stones and have the means to display it during the assembly (check copyright).
- Note that, to allow adequate time for involvement and reflection, this material could be used in a number of shorter assemblies.

 Assembly

1. Welcome everyone to the last week of term and introduce the theme of stepping stones. Explain that, when there is no bridge, stepping stones provide a way across a shallow river. Invite two or three children to cross the stepping stones you have constructed, 'one step at a time'.

2. Go on to explain that, because stepping stones must be crossed in this manner, they are often used to describe the way in which new skills and understanding are gained – one step at a time. They also are a good image to use for making progress through life.

3. Reflect that stepping stones can be a challenge. Sometimes they are wet and slippery, sometimes they seem a long way apart. It can be difficult to keep our balance. The encouragement and help of friends can mean a lot. Invite a number of children to cross the stepping stones in line together. Note that we need to be thankful for friends who lend a helping hand.

4. Invite the children to use the stepping stones to celebrate the changes and achievement of the past year. Nominate someone to cross the stones – one step at a time – as members of their class recall some of the things that have been enjoyed and learned. Mention that we should be thankful for steps that lead to new experiences and understanding.

5. Reflect that many children will soon be moving on to new classes – even new schools. Ask everyone how they feel about facing change. Observe that a range of emotions (and some anxiety) is only natural. Suggest that remembering our past achievements can help us to move on to enjoy further success. Encourage the children to have positive attitudes, declaring, 'I can', 'I will', 'I dare', 'I believe', 'I'll try', 'I'll succeed', as they cross the stepping stones, one step at a time.

   Church schools, in addition, might reflect on the role of faith when facing change. Recall that, when the time came for Jesus to leave his friends, he asked them to remember what they had learned from him and share his message with people all over the world. It was a big step, so, to help his friends, Jesus said, 'Remember, I am with you always' (Matthew 28.20). You could invite some of the children to cross the stepping stones, repeating the text, a stepping stone at a time.

 Time for reflection

Be thankful for the stepping stones of life:

- for past achievements and the challenges that lie ahead
- for good friends and helping hands
- for new opportunities and the excitement of moving on together . . . one step at a time.

Prayer

Lord Jesus,
Thank you for your promise: 'Remember, I am with you always'.
Help us to know that to be true – yesterday, today and for ever.
Amen.

Leavers' blessing

We wish you well for the future.
Take pride in yourself.
Think of others.
Aim to do good.
Dream dreams.
Don't be discouraged.
Believe and be strong.
May the blessings of life
and the blessings of God
be yours today and always.
Amen.

 Song

'One more step along the world I go' (*Come and Praise*, 47)

FOR ANY SEASON

A BUNCH OF BANANAS

Suitable for Whole School

 Aim

To reflect on the importance of positive attitudes and outlook within the school community.

 Preparation and materials

- You will need a smiley face (yours!), a bunch of yellow bananas and another single curved banana.
- If used early in the school year, in the 'Assembly', Step 2, below, you could make reference to smiles being a sign of welcome and Step 3 might be expanded to recognize that the experience of being new is challenging and existing class members can help newcomers to feel a part of their year group.

 Assembly

1. Begin brightly and cheerfully by saying that you'd like to invite everybody to think and act positively throughout the coming day/week/term/year.

2. Introduce the focus for the assembly – a bunch of bananas. Respond to any amusement by recognizing that, while 'going bananas' is a phrase describing someone who is rather silly, you have some serious points to make, but in a fun way!

3. *Hold up the bunch of bananas.*

   Point out that a bunch of bananas is bright and cheerful. Bananas are yellow – a happy and positive colour. Bananas also grow in the shape of a smile.

   Hold the single curved banana in front of your face curving upwards so it looks like a smiling mouth.

   Reflect that everyone learns and works best in a happy atmosphere. Those who bring a smile to school bring great encouragement to others.

4. Should anything happen to make us feel glum *(invert banana to make a sad face)*, that's when another smiling face and listening ear can do so much to help.

   Turn banana to make a happy face as before. If your school has a 'buddy' scheme this might be referred to briefly here.

5. Reflect that bananas grow together in large bunches, divided into clusters called 'hands'. School is a place where everyone (young and old) learns together. Each class is a place where different people can belong. Which class will prove to be the best and most helpful *bunch*? Where are the helping *hands*? When friendships are under strain, will you *hang* together?

6. Observe that bananas give us energy. We need lots of energy to learn and really enjoy school. Some energy is physical – provided by a good night's sleep, healthy breakfast (not to be missed!) and, perhaps, a banana for a mid-morning snack! Other energy is spiritual – flowing from our love of God, other people and the world around us. Express the hope that members of the school community will approach every task and challenge with energy and enthusiasm.

7. In a final reference to the fruit, conclude by saying that everyone will now see that you haven't gone completely bananas! It's simply that it sums up the enjoyment of being part of a cheerful, united and energetic school community. With such thoughts in mind, wish everybody a great 'bunch of bananas' day!

 Time for reflection

Invite everyone to take time to think and pray.

Think why it is good to be alive . . . and smile.

Think of friends you enjoy being with . . . and be thankful.

Think of all today will hold . . . and get excited about it!

Church schools may also wish to reflect on Paul's fruits of God's Spirit (Galatians 5.22–23):

> *The fruit of the Spirit is love, joy, peace, patience, kindness, generosity, faithfulness, gentleness, and self-control.*

> *Prayer*
> Lord God,
> You give to us . . .
> the joy of being alive,
> the company of others,
> the opportunities of each new day.
> Bless this school community and each and every member of it,
> today and always.
> **Amen.**

 Song

'Wake up!' or 'Today' (*Songs for Every Assembly*, Out of the Ark Music, 1999)

A CHAIN OF THANKS

Suitable for Whole School

Aim

To understand the importance of saying 'Thank you'.

Preparation and materials

- You will need six rubber quoits or small hula hoops, each with a laminated label with the words 'Thank you' or 'Thanks' secured to them across the middle by means of short cable ties or string. The advantage of the hula hoops is that they provide more space for the words.
- You will also need eight children to take part in the story in the 'Assembly', Step 3, below.
- You can use the script provided or these children, or a class, might like to prepare their own version.
- Other children could role-play the opening conversations in the 'Assembly', Step 1, but this is optional.

Assembly

1. Invite the children to consider some short conversations. What word or phrase is missing from each?

   Dean is given a birthday present by his parents.

   Parent: Happy birthday, Dean. We hope you like it.
   Dean (unwrapping the present): Wow! It's an Xbox! Let's get it set up!

   Sedika offers to help Katy who is struggling to put her coat on before going out to play.

   Sedika: Let me help, Katy. You've got your coat arm inside out!
   Katy: No, I can do it myself. Stupid coat!

   It's the end of Dance Club, which is held on Wednesday lunchtime by Miss Canham. Everyone has had a good time, including Lucy and Priya.

   Miss Canham: Well done everyone! Time to get back to our afternoon lessons now.
   Lucy (to Priya): Come on, let's get changed.

2. Hopefully, someone will spot that the missing phrase is 'Thank you'! Invite everyone to consider why saying 'Thank you' is important. Reflect that:
   - saying 'Thank you' shows that you value another person
   - saying 'Thank you' brings out the best in others
   - saying 'Thank you' draws people closer together
   - saying 'Thank you' shows you are part of a team or family.

3. Say that you will illustrate this by telling a story about how one chain of thanks was created. Proceed along the following lines using your eight helpers' real names in place of the ones here.

   A chain of thanks

   Here are Jude and Rajan. Rajan had lots of bags to carry in to school and Jude helped by carrying one. Rajan said, 'Thank you'.

Produce the first 'Thank you' quoit or hoop for Jude and Rajan to hold between them, forming the first link in the chain.

Jude was pleased to be Rajan's friend.

As they went into their class, Sian held open the door. *(Sian joins the two boys.)* 'Thank you,' said Jude.

Produce second 'Thank you' quoit or hoop for Sian and Jude to hold between them.

'That's fine,' said Sian.

'Would you like me to hand out the books?' Sian said to the class teacher, Mr Abrahams. 'Thank you,' he replied. 'That would be good.'

Sian and Mr Abrahams hold the third 'Thank you' quoit or hoop.

Later, Becky didn't understand her work. Mr Abrahams came to her table and explained what she had to do. 'I see now,' said Becky. 'Thank you very much.'

Becky and Mr Abrahams hold the fourth 'Thank you' quoit or hoop.

Pause at this point to ensure the children understand the point that is being made. The chain of thanks shows people being joined together to become a caring class and a strong team. Reinforce the points made in Step 2.

Continue the story by joining others to the chain, as follows, for example.

At playtime, Becky was alone and Ingrid came to ask if she wanted to join in a game. 'Thank you,' she replied. 'I'd like that a lot.'

Ingrid and Becky hold the fifth 'Thank you' quoit or hoop.

After the bell rang and everyone went inside, Ingrid couldn't find her bag. It had fallen from her peg. Sam helped her to find it and she was very relieved. 'Thanks, Sam,' she said.

Sam and Ingrid hold the sixth 'Thank you' quoit or hoop.

Reiterate the point that saying 'Thank you' creates a strong and close sense of belonging. Stress that forgetting to say 'Thank you' will discourage others from helping and break the chain! Conclude by challenging everyone to become part of a chain of thanks.

4. Church schools may wish to refer to a phrase from Paul's letter to the Ephesians (1.16, GNB):

   'I have not stopped giving thanks to God for you.'

Even the most important people mustn't forget to say 'Thank you' to those who help them.

 Time for reflection

Invite everyone to think of another person who has helped them today.

Did they remember to say 'Thank you'?

Suggest that everyone might consider how to help others in turn.

Invite everyone to resolve and pray to bring out the best in others.

 Songs

'Thank you, Lord' (*Songs for Every Singing School*, Out of the Ark Music, 2004; suitable for an end of day assembly)

'Thank you, Lord, for this new day' (*Come and Praise*, 32; include as a verse 'Thank you, Lord, for friends who care')

A PERFECT PICTURE

Suitable for Whole School

 Aims

To celebrate how painting and colour can express human moods and values.

 Preparation and materials

- You will need some art materials – paper, paints, brushes and so on – and a table to display them on.
- Invite members of a Reception or Key Stage 1 class to bring some of their paintings to the assembly. Equally, if Key Stage 2 children are studying the work of a particular artist, this could provide an opportunity for them to present some of their pictures. Alternatively, find an image of one your favourite paintings and have the means available to display it during the assembly.
- Learn the song 'I'm going to paint a perfect picture' (*Come and Praise*, 83).

 Assembly

1. Place the art materials on the table, to act as a point of focus. Explain that there are different kinds of paint, such as watercolour, oils, acrylic. Watercolours are used on paper, oils require a stiff canvas. Colours can be mixed on a paint tray or palette. Does anyone know how to make the colour . . . (run through various colours)? There are large and small brushes, some hard and others soft, some thick and others fine, each used at different times for different parts of the painting.

2. Suggest that such bright and varied materials might make anyone want to paint a picture. Say, 'I'd like to paint a picture', but then ask, 'What shall I paint?' Invite suggestions from the children. What would they paint?

3. Introduce the Reception or Key Stage 1 children's paintings or the Key Stage 2 children's work, if available. Discuss the use of colour and choices of subject, the mood that a painting can evoke.

4. Alternatively show the image of your chosen painting and explain why it is a favourite.

5. Reflect that painting has always been important to human beings. Thousands of years ago, when people lived in caves, they painted pictures on the walls showing the animals that they hunted (cave art). Beautiful paintings have been found decorating Egyptian tombs. For many centuries in Europe, artists were employed by the Church and they painted religious subjects, but, as time has passed, a greater variety of styles and subjects has developed. Paintings of people are called 'portraits' and those of the countryside are 'landscapes'. Some paintings reflect experiences of war and suffering (images we often see on television today). Others show scenes of beauty and happiness.

6. Invite the children to consider what kind of world they would like to paint and introduce the song 'I'm going to paint a perfect picture'.

Time for reflection

Invite the children to close their eyes and imagine their perfect picture.

> *Prayer*
>
> Lord God of shape and colour,
> We celebrate your bright and vibrant world.
> Blend our lives together so that we can add to its beauty
> and live together in harmony,
> today and every day.
> **Amen.**

 Songs

'I'm going to paint a perfect picture' (*Come and Praise*, 83)

'Everywhere around me' (*Songs for Every Assembly*, Out of the Ark Music, 1999)

A TALE OF TWO SISTERS

Suitable for Whole School

 Aim

To affirm that we are all different and all have a place in school and our families.

 Preparation and materials

- Familiarize yourself with the narrative set out in the 'Assembly', Step 2, below, which could also be effectively presented using three voices.
- You will need a leader, plus two other adults or children to read the parts of Martha and Mary in Step 2 if you opt to present the assembly using three voices.
- A focus table could be set up, contrasting some pots and pans with a small pile of books.

 Assembly

1. Invite the children to quietly reflect on when they last argued with a brother, sister or friend. Observe that, from time to time, disagreements happen. Not everyone is the same. Sometimes an argument arises over a task that needs to be done.

2. Introduce the Bible story below, which is about two sisters. They shared the same home (with their brother Lazarus), but had very different personalities. Invite the children to listen carefully. Which of the sisters are they most like?

   A tale of two sisters

Martha loved to keep busy.	Mary loved to think.
Martha could be very impatient.	Mary was very calm.
Martha loved cooking.	Mary didn't!

   So, when Martha and Mary invited Jesus to their home, this happened:

Martha laid the table.	Mary sat on the floor.
Martha watched the oven.	Mary listened to Jesus.
Martha cooked the dinner.	Mary didn't!
Martha was hot in the kitchen.	Mary stayed in the cool.
A pot boiled over.	Mary didn't realize.

   Finally, Martha's anger boiled over too! 'Mary, what kind of sister are you? Jesus, tell her to come and help me!'

   'Martha,' Jesus replied, 'I know you're upset, but Mary is enjoying a special time that she'll always remember.'

   So Martha returned to her cooking . . . Mary carried on listening.

3. Allow the children to respond to the story . . . What advice would they offer to Martha and Mary? Did Mary eventually help Martha to serve her special meal and to clear up afterwards? Was her sister's plea for help ignored?

4. Observe that this story reflects the frustration we feel when people don't behave in accordance with our wishes or do what we feel they should do. Explain that strong friendships allow others the freedom to be themselves. However, such friendships also mean being sensitive to one another's feelings and being ready

to help. As Martha and Mary discovered, this balance can sometimes be difficult to keep. Jesus encouraged the two sisters to understand their different gifts and needs.

 Time for reflection

Invite the children to reflect on how both helping *and* listening will be/have been important in their school day.

Prayer

Lord God,
Sometimes we get cross and frustrated with our sisters, brothers and friends.
We're sorry for the occasions when we lose our tempers.
Help us to think about the feelings of others, allow one another space and offer help when we can.
Amen.

 Songs

'We're here again' (*Songs for Every Singing School*, Out of the Ark Music, 2004)
'Kum ba yah' (*Come and Praise*, 68)

ALL FROM ONE SMALL PIP!

Suitable for Whole School

 Aim

To celebrate the potential of small beginnings.

 Preparation and materials

- You will need some large Bramley cooking apples, plus a corer, knife and peeler.
- If yours is a church school, you might like to include the parable of the mustard seed in Matthew 13, given in the 'Assembly', Step 4, below. Familiarize yourself with the story and the accompanying ideas and actions so that you can get the children to join in. An alternative, using the same actions, is given in Step 5.

 Assembly

1. Display the Bramley apples. Invite the children to note that they are bigger than many other apples. Observe that such apples can be very sour. Explain that this is because they are cooking apples. They are peeled, cored and sliced, sweetened with sugar and put into pies or crumbles. Demonstrate how an apple is prepared and point out that the small 'pips' are seeds.

2. Continue by telling the story of how these large apples, a variety called *Bramley* apples, were first grown over 200 years ago in 1809 – starting from a very small beginning.

   From one small pip

   Mary's mother carefully placed the apple pie in the simple oven in the cottage where they lived. She wiped her floury hands. 'That's all the baking done, Mary. Now let's clear away.'

   Mary Brailsford, who was 18, gathered up the remains of the apples she had prepared. Among the curls of green apple peel were pieces of the core and some dark brown pips.

   'I wonder,' she said, 'if these will grow.'

   'You can try,' her mother replied. 'We may be lucky, but it will be a long time before we have any apples from them to make a pie!'

   Outside, in the cottage garden, Mary found a small pot, filled it with earth and planted the pips, one by one. She stood the pot on the kitchen windowsill.

   Later that spring, Mary was pleased to find a small, two-leaved seedling in her pot. One of the apple pips she had sown had grown! As it grew larger, she found it a bigger pot and, many baking days later, planted it in a sunny corner of the garden.

   Eventually, she married and left the cottage where she had grown up. She had forgotten about the apple pip until, one day, her mother visited and brought her an apple pie. 'I hope you enjoy it, Mary. I've made it with some of the apples that have grown on your tree!' Mary was surprised! It astounded her to think that the small pip she had planted was now a tree producing apples of its own!

   Years later, a newcomer called Mr Bramley came to live at the cottage where the apple tree still grew. By now, Mary's tree was producing so many apples that many were given away to friends and neighbours. One day, they caught the attention of a man called Mr Merryweather. His family grew the fruit trees that were planted in orchards and gardens. 'These are very fine apples,' he remarked. 'I've never seen this kind before. Could I take some cuttings to see if we can grow some more?'

'Of course,' replied Mr Bramley, 'but (he chuckled) you must promise me one thing! Please will you call the apples Bramley, after me? I'd like my name to be famous!'

'We'll have to do our best to get these to grow then!' replied Mr Merryweather as he carefully cut some shoots from the tree.

The shoots grew! Soon, more and more trees were producing the large cooking apples that became known as 'Bramley's Seedling'. They were the very best cooking apples. News of their quality spread and Bramley apples were the ones that people wanted to put in their pies.

Mr Merryweather sold hundreds of Bramley apple trees. Soon they could be found in orchards and cottage gardens all over Britain. The name Bramley was famous! Mr Merryweather, however, wanted to make sure that someone else was not forgotten, so he also told the story of how Mary first planted her apple pip. 'Isn't it amazing,' he said, 'that so many people can enjoy these wonderful apples that have all grown from one small pip!'

The story *is* amazing! The apple tree that Mary grew still stands in the garden of the cottage that was her home. It's now very old, but still bears fruit. The name Bramley remains famous, too, because the Bramley apples that grew from Mary's pip are still the best for baking and putting into pies!

3. Observe that the story illustrates the importance of small beginnings and the miracle of harvest. That Mary's tiny pip grew has meant fantastic crops of apples have been produced year after year and brought enjoyment to lots and lots of people. Small beginnings can bear much fruit.

4. Church schools may wish to link this story to the parable (picture story) of the mustard seed Jesus told (Matthew 13). Prepare the children so that they can think about and make the following appropriate actions and responses to different words and phrases used in the story.

   - When the word 'seed' is mentioned, they are to imagine placing a seed in the ground and exclaim, **'So small!'**
   - Depict growth by linking your thumbs and outstretching your fingers to form two leaves. Then lift your arms high to form a tree, exclaiming, **'How tall!'**
   - Extend your arms wide in a circle, concluding, **'For all!'**

   Jesus' parable of a tiny seed
   Jesus said, God's pattern for life is like this.
   Once a man sowed a tiny seed. **'So small!'**
   It grew and grew into a large tree. **'How tall!'**
   The tree became so large that lots of birds came to nest in its branches. **'For all!'**

5. Alternatively, rehearse the story of the Bramley apple seed and actions in the same way as given in Step 4, above, but with the following wording.

   The tiny Bramley apple seed
   Let's celebrate life's pattern.
   Once a girl sowed a tiny seed. **'So small!'**
   It grew and grew into a large tree. **'How tall!'**
   The tree became so large, lots of people enjoyed the fruit that grew on its branches. **'For all!'**

Time for reflection

Invite everyone to spend some moments thinking about the story and the importance of small beginnings.

What beginnings might you make today?
Like Mary, will you act on the seed of an idea?
Like Mr Merryweather, will you make the most of a small opportunity?
Like Mr Bramley, will you be willing to share?

Prayer

Creator God,
We thank you today for the fruits of the earth
and the fruits of thoughtfulness, giving, patience and care.
Amen.

DEALING WITH DISAPPOINTMENT

Suitable for Key Stage 2

Aim

To explore our responses to sporting disappointment.

Preparation and materials

- This assembly is suitable for general use or can be used as a response to national or local sporting disappointment.
- Prepare two sets of key words:
  - upset, angry, useless, ashamed
  - think, change, remember, support

  and have the means to display them clearly and appropriately – perhaps in team colours, with a national flag or drawn from a kit bag. This assembly was originally a response to England's elimination from European and World Football Tournaments and the key words were displayed on the four quarters of an image of the St George's Flag.

Assembly

1. If the assembly is being used as a response to a specific sporting disappointment, refer to the events reported in the news. Reflect on the feelings of the athletes or players involved and their supporters.

2. Alternatively, invite the children to consider one or both of the following scenarios. How would they feel?

   - Imagine that you are a runner. You are one of the best runners in the UK and so won a place on the Olympic team. You've spent the past year preparing for your event, but, just before the Games, you injured yourself in training. The race has just ended. You took part, but, due to your injury, had to drop out before the end. This was the experience of Paula Radcliffe, long distance runner, during the 2004 Olympic Games.
   - Imagine that you are in a Premier League football team. You've had a great season and are second in the League. Your team has also won a place in the final of the FA Cup. Everybody expects that you will win. The opposition team is at the bottom of the League. At full-time the score is still 0-0. Then, a few seconds into stoppage time, the other side scores a goal. Shortly afterwards, the referee blows the final whistle and you realize your team's been beaten. This was the experience of Manchester City in the 2013 FA Cup Final.

3. Sum up the discussion, producing the first set of key words. Disappointment can leave us feeling:

   - *upset* – when we lose something we want very much indeed, naturally we feel unhappy and tearful
   - *angry* – we look for other people to blame or blame ourselves
   - *useless* – we may be tempted to give in, thinking that we will never succeed
   - *ashamed* – we may worry what other people think of us.

4. Invite the children to consider how those concerned might deal with this disappointment. Produce the second set of key words:
   - *think* – although it is painful, we have to face up to our disappointments and try to learn from them
   - *remember* – we can find encouragement in remembering our strengths – it's not helpful to think only of our mistakes when we know that we can do so many things well
   - *change* – when we have not succeeded, we must establish new aims and goals and may need to try a different approach
   - *support* – teamwork is important – we all need support and understanding (not unfriendly criticism) if we are to deal with disappointment. Will supporters continue to encourage the athlete or team?

5. Conclude that the many different disappointments we experience needn't destroy us. Learning to deal with disappointment can help us to become stronger people. Invite the children to listen to how Paul wrote about his difficulties and disappointments (in 2 Corinthians 4.8–9 and 16, GNB):

   We are often troubled, but not crushed; sometimes in doubt, but never in despair; there are many enemies, but we are never without a friend; and though badly hurt at times, we are not destroyed . . . For this reason we never become discouraged.

 Time for reflection

Prayer
Lord God,
When we feel fed up and discouraged,
give us the insights and strength we need
to deal with disappointment.
Amen.

 Songs

'Together' (*Songs for Every Occasion*, Out of the Ark Music, 2002)

'Give us hope, Lord' (*Come and Praise*, 87)

INCY WINCY SPIDER

Suitable for Key Stage 1

Aims

To show the importance of perseverance and resilience in attaining goals.

Preparation and materials

- You will need two sets of Jenga building blocks or other suitable building materials.
- If you don't know them already, familiarize yourself with the words and actions of the song 'Incy Wincy spider'.
- A video of 'Incy Wincy spider' can be found at <http://learnenglishkids.britishcouncil.org/en/songs/incy-wincy-spider>. You might like to play it at the end of the assembly and all sing along, doing the actions.
- You will also need two readers or a group to read the conversation in the 'Time for reflection' section, below. Practise it a few times before the assembly so it flows well.

Assembly

1. Introduce the building materials with the thought, 'I wonder who might build the highest tower?'

2. Invite two children to build towers, emphasizing that the goal (or aim) is to construct the tallest tower. Consider how the materials might be arranged differently to strengthen the structure and increase the height.

   Commiserate should a tower fall and encourage another attempt. Congratulate the participants and affirm their readiness to try.

3. Explain that the task presented a challenge. A challenge isn't easy. It tests our skill and patience. If we are to succeed with a challenge, we need to keep trying.

4. Refer to a song about a character who aimed high and kept trying.

   Enjoy singing (with actions) 'Incy Wincy spider'.

   Reflect that, even when Incy Wincy's adventure didn't go according to plan, Incy Wincy didn't give in.

5. Identify some of the challenges that the children face in school. Some goals aren't easily reached and at times everyone feels down and disappointed, but there's encouragement in the example of Incy Wincy spider!

6. Introduce another verse to the song, using the same actions.

   When you face a challenge, do the best you can.
   We all feel down when things don't go to plan.
   Look on the bright side. Have another try.
   Be like Incy Wincy and keep on aiming high!

Time for reflection

> *Reader 1*: A water spout is so tall and a spider is so small!
> *Reader 2*: Up we go!
> *Reader 1*: It's dark in here.

Reader 2: Look up – you can see the sky!

Reader 1: It's getting dark, I think it might rain.

Together: Oh no! It is raining!

Reader 1: Are you all right?

Reader 2: I think so.

Reader 1: What shall we do now?

Reader 2: Well, the sun's come out.

Together: Let's try again!

Prayer

Dear Lord,
When at first we don't succeed,
help us to try, try again.
Amen.

 Song

'One more step along the world I go' (*Come and Praise*, 47)

The assembly might be concluded with the video clip of 'Incy Wincy spider'.

JUST A LITTLE BIT

Suitable for Whole School

Aim

To show the need for thoughtfulness and self-restraint.

Preparation and materials

- You will need a freshly baked full-length baguette and a good appetite!
- Familiarize yourself with the story in the 'Assembly', Step 2, below, and note that you will need the help of eight children. You could, as outlined in Step 2, just select children on the day or prepare them a little more in advance, as you prefer.

Assembly

1. Produce the baguette. Reflect that it smells good. Suggest that it might be all right to eat some – 'just a little bit'. Savour a small piece and wonder if you might try some more – 'just a little bit' – but then resist this temptation, saying, 'I might not know when to stop.' Explain that 'knowing when to stop' is the theme of the assembly.

2. Ask who enjoys eating bread and enlist the help of eight children, to become a sister, three friends and four ducks.

   Tell and enact the story, along the following lines, acting the part in the story of Liam yourself. As the narrative proceeds, break off pieces of bread at the appropriate points to share with the other characters – just a little bit!

   ### Just a little bit

   Liam's tummy told him that it was almost teatime. His mum was cooking some spaghetti bolognaise. It was Liam's favourite meal.

   'Are we going to have some crusty bread with it?' he asked. His mother had forgotten to buy the bread that Liam liked. The supermarket was only a short distance away through the park, so Liam and his sister, Anna, were often sent to get things when they were needed. Liam and Anna went to buy some bread.

   They paid at the supermarket checkout and went back outside into the sunshine. The baguette was still warm from the oven.

   'Mmm,' said Liam, 'this does smell good. Shall we taste some? Just a little bit! Mum won't mind.' They both tore a piece off. It tasted lovely. Liam realized how hungry he felt. 'I could eat some more. Just a little bit! Could you Anna?' They sat together on a park bench and happily ate 'just a little bit' more.

   Three friends – Jordan, Ashleigh and April – joined them.

   'That bread does look nice,' April said. 'Could we each have some?'

   'Well . . . ,' Liam wondered for a moment. 'Yes . . . of course . . . but just a little bit!'

   The path through the park went past the lake, where there were more hungry friends. A crowd of hungry ducks saw the bag that Liam was carrying. They ran across the grass, quacking furiously.

   'O bless!' laughed Anna. 'Liam, let's feed them. Give me some bread – just a little bit.' Together, they fed the ducks and also themselves! (Just a little bit.)

3. You can imagine what happened. When Liam and Anna got home, there was very little of the baguette left! Their mum was rather cross, but not for long when Liam and Anna told her what had happened. Liam was sad, not because of anything that was said, but because now he was so full up, he hadn't left enough room in his tummy to enjoy his favourite meal.

4. Invite the children to reflect on the story. What had led Liam and Anna to eat so much of the bread? Focus on the phrase 'just a little bit'. Liam told himself that 'just a little bit' didn't matter, but, bit by bit, more and more of the baguette was eaten!

5. Conclude by reflecting on the thought that small choices, though small, matter.

   Other examples might be given:
   - lots of small mistakes can have a big impact on the quality of a piece of work
   - repeated name-calling isn't a little thing, it's a sign of a big bully
   - stealing small things is still stealing and can lead to big trouble.

   It's important to think about the consequences of our actions. Small mistakes can become bigger ones if we pretend that they don't matter.

 Time for reflection

A time of reflection might be based on the ideas in the following prayer.

> *Prayer*
> Loving God,
> Sometimes we imagine small choices don't matter,
> but they can mean a lot.
> When we say to ourselves, 'It's just a little thing',
> help us to remember that little things can add up in a big way.
> Happiness so often depends on a little bit of care – a little bit of thought.
> **Amen.**

 Songs

'The Lord's Prayer' (*Come and Praise*, 51)

'Rejoice in the Lord always' (*Come and Praise*, 95)

ONE BODY, MANY PARTS

Suitable for Key Stage 2

 Aim

To be aware that different parts of our bodies have different functions and the need to coordinate efforts and endeavours.

 Preparation and materials

- Create a visual of the words to the song 'Head, shoulders, knees and toes' and have the means to display it during the assembly.

 Assembly

1. Begin by asking, 'Are we all here?' . . . 'Is every part of us here?' Suggest that everyone makes sure by singing 'Head, shoulders, knees and toes'.

   Display the words to 'Head, shoulders, knees and toes'.

   Head, shoulders, knees and toes, knees and toes,
   Head, shoulders, knees and toes, knees and toes,
   And eyes and ears, and mouth and nose,
   Head, shoulders, knees and toes, knees and toes.

   Invite the children to do the actions, touching the parts of their bodies as they're mentioned in the song. Increase the pace of the singing and keep trying to do the actions in time with the words. Observe that it's not always easy to keep different parts working together!

2. Invite everyone to consider how movements are coordinated. Establish that parts of our bodies must work together when we write, kick a ball, sing a song, cook a meal, play a musical instrument.

3. Suggest that there is a lesson here. Like the various parts of a human body, different *people* have different skills and abilities. To achieve their goals, the individuals within any group (or body) of people need to work together.

4. Invite everyone to listen to some words from the Bible (1 Corinthians 12.14–20, GNB) about working together. Suggest the following actions for whenever the following words are said:

   - for the word 'body', flex biceps
   - for the word 'one', raise an index finger
   - for 'many parts', raise and wiggle all your fingers
   - for 'foot', 'hand', 'eye' and 'ear', point to each on your bodies.

     The body . . . is not made up of only one part, but of many parts. If the foot were to say, 'Because I am not a hand, I don't belong to the body,' that would not keep it from being a part of the body. And if the ear were to say, 'Because I am not an eye, I don't belong to the body,' that would not keep it from being a part of the body. If the whole body were just an eye, how could it hear? And if it were only an ear, how could it smell? . . . God put every different part in the body just as he wanted it to be. There would not be a body if it were only one part! As it is, there are many parts but one body.

5. Congratulate everyone who has joined in. Introduce a second verse to the original song that echoes the Bible phrase, 'there are many parts but one body'. This time, use the same actions as before for the words 'body', 'one', 'many parts', 'eyes' and 'ears', but add the following:

   – for 'hands', raise both hands in the air
   – for 'hearts', put both hands on your chest.

   Conclude that the life of any community is happiest and most successful when everyone works together and tries to help one another.

   One body, many parts, many parts,
   One body, many parts, many parts,
   Eyes and ears and hands and hearts,
   One body, many parts.

 Time for reflection

Invite everyone to consider how working together will be important in the day that lies ahead.

Prayer

Loving God,
Thank you that each one of us is special and, working together, we can do so much more than we can ever do alone.
Amen.

PEACE BABIES

Suitable for Whole School

Aim

To celebrate peace and peacemaking.

Preparation and resources

- You will need a packet of Bassett's Jelly Babies – they must be Bassett's.
- You will also need a flipchart or whiteboard and markers in different colours, like the Jelly Babies.
- Prepare the text from Matthew 5.9 (GNB) and have the means to display it during the 'Assembly', Step 6, below.
- If you are using this for a class assembly and would like to pass the sweets around, ensure that you have first checked if any of the children have allergies to any of the ingredients – and that you have an adequate supply!

Assembly

1. Produce the packet of Jelly Babies. Identify the different colours and flavours – strawberry, lime, blackcurrant, lemon, raspberry and orange. Which are most popular? You could conduct a quick opinion poll.

2. Explain that Jelly Babies were first launched in 1918 to celebrate the end of the First World War. They were called 'Peace Babies' and quickly became popular. During the Second World War, production ceased because of a shortage of ingredients. They were 'reborn' in 1953, with the new name of 'Jelly Babies'.

3. Invite the children to consider why the sale of Jelly Babies was a good way to celebrate peace. Reflect that the Peace Babies marked a new beginning. They showed that life was returning to normal and could be fun again.

4. Explain that each of the six 'babies' has a name and an identity. Refer to the illustrations on the Bassett's packaging.
   - Pink Baby Bonny, wears a nappy and frilly bonnet. She is always crawling into mischief!
   - Boofuls is green, soft-hearted and cries a lot, even when he is happy!
   - Bumper is orange, wears a bumbag and bumps into things!
   - Bubbles has her hair in a ponytail and is yellow.
   - Bigheart is black and always puts his friends first.
   - Brilliant is the red leader of the gang.

5. Peace is enjoyed when people of different ages, interests and appearances live together in harmony. Think about it, wouldn't a bag of Jelly Babies be dull if the sweets were all one colour and flavour?

6. Suggest that there's a sense in which we all can be 'Peace Babies'.
   Display the text from Matthew 5.9 (GNB).

   Happy are those who work for peace; God will call them his children!

7. Invite everyone to consider how they can 'work for peace'. Write the suggestions on to the flipchart or whiteboard using the different colours.

Refer back to the bag of sweets. Working for peace doesn't mean being soft, like a Jelly Baby. It calls for a strong commitment to friendship, being ready to share and celebrating the good things of life together.

8. If doing so, pass the sweets around (taking into account any allergies you're aware of) and invite everyone to enjoy a Peace Baby!

 Time for reflection

Prayer

Loving God,
Help us to work for peace,
and pray for peace,
believing that all people are your children.
Amen.

 Song

'Let the world rejoice' (*Come and Praise*, 148)

WALKING IN THE RAIN

Suitable for Reception and Key Stage 1

Aim

To give thanks for rain and recognize that water is vital for life.

Preparation and materials

- You will need your raincoat, hat and wellington boots.

Assembly

1. Observe that most people dislike rainy days. Wet weather can certainly disrupt outdoor activities, but rain is essential to life on planet Earth.

2. Invite the children to join in an imaginary rainy day walk. Put on your wet weather gear and proceed along the following lines, encouraging everyone to use all their senses. Take your time and allow the children to contribute to the role play and take in each of the following sensory aspects of the experience of rain.

   - *Listen*, it's raining! Can you hear the raindrops beating against the window and drumming on the roof? Let's put on our raincoats and go outside. Can you hear other sounds that the rain makes? Splish on to the leaves and splash into puddles. It's gurgling down gutters.
   - Take a deep breath. What can you *smell*? Is it the scent of flowers, damp leaves, even the muddy soil? Rain washes and refreshes everything. The world around us would be very dusty without rain. We would be very dusty and dirty, too! Rain provides water for us to wash our clothes and bodies.
   - *Feel* the rain on your face. It falls from grey clouds. It's warm and gentle. Will the weather become stormy? What will the clouds look like then? How will that rain feel? Let's be thankful for the clothes that keep us warm and dry. Think of people who work outside in all weathers.
   - *Look* at the rain making bubbles in the puddles and streaming down the gutter in the road. It's disappearing down drains. Where will it go? The rain will find its way into streams and rivers and, eventually, the sea! Some will be dried up by the sun and make new clouds. Much of the rain soaks into the soil and is sucked up by the roots of trees and plants. Look at them growing! Without rain they would die.
   - Stick out your tongues to see if the rain has any *taste*. It's pure and clear. It's gathered in big lakes called reservoirs. It becomes the water that's piped to our homes. Like plants, we need to drink lots of water. It's good for us. Without it we, too, would die.

3. Finish by observing that it's good to get back into the dry! Discard your wet weather gear and invite the children to reflect what they have learned about the importance of rain. Stress that rain brings life!

Time for reflection

Invite the children to pause for prayer and reflection, holding their hands palms uppermost, as if to feel for rain.

Prayer

Lord,
Let's be thankful for . . .
the senses that help us to enjoy and explore the Earth.
Let's be thankful for . . .
refreshing rain, the water of life.
Amen.

 Songs

The words of 'Thank you, Lord, for this new day' (*Come and Praise*, 32) could be freely
adapted, as I have here.

Thank you, Lord, for rainy days,
Thank you, Lord, for rainy days,
Thank you, Lord, for rainy days,
Here at *(name)* school. *or* Right where we are.

Pitter, patter, splish, splash, splosh, *
Pitter, patter, splish, splash, splosh,
Pitter, patter, splish, splash, splosh,
Sing a song of rain!

Thank you, Lord, for wellie boots (repeat × 3)
For jumping through the puddles!

Thank you, Lord, for flowers and plants (repeat × 3)
Growing green and tall!

Thank you, Lord, for streams and rivers (repeat × 3)
Flowing to the sea!

Thank you, Lord, for pure clean water (repeat × 3)
To wash and cook and drink.

'It's always wet' (*Wonderful Water*, Out of the Ark Music, 2007)

'Wet, wet, wet' (*It Must be Spring*, Out of the Ark Music, 2001)

---

*The words of this line could be split and sung by different groups.

WHEN TEARS FLOW

Suitable for Key Stage 2

Aim

To understand how different emotions are expressed in tears.

Preparation and materials

- You will need an onion, knife, chopping board and box of tissues for the introduction, in the 'Assembly', Step 1, below, but see also the next point.
- Material from this assembly could be adapted to respond to an item of national news or at a time of loss within the school community. In such cases, the introduction can be changed to refer to these events, with Step 1 omitted and so the materials above would not be needed. An image of a rainbow could be displayed.
- It would be appropriate for church schools to use this material during Lent, concluding with a reading of John 11.28–29 and 31–36.

Assembly

1. Begin to peel and chop the onion. Observe that it's not easy to prepare an onion without crying. A strong substance is released that causes the tear ducts in our eyes to water.

2. Carefully wipe your eyes with the tissues and refer to the fact that strong emotions (or feelings) also cause tears. Explain that crying is sometimes considered babyish or silly, but, like laughter, tears simply reflect our inmost feelings. People of all ages cry. Some are moved to tears very easily. Others keep their feelings hidden.

3. Reflect that tears flow as a result of feeling a wide range of emotions. Illustrate this by reference to sport.
   - Winning athletes on the podium are sometimes moved to tears as their national anthem is played. Why? Establish that these are tears of happiness, pride and relief at their achievement.
   - Tears also flow when athletes are injured or defeated. Establish that these are tears of disappointment, pain and frustration.

4. Gently explain that, as some of the children will know, tears are also shed when something sad has happened. Perhaps a friend or family member has moved away, is sick or has died. Tears arise not just from sadness but also from happy memories of friendship that has been shared together. Often tears and laughter mingle together – we can find something so funny we end up crying with laughter!

5. Assure everyone that it's all right to cry. Tears let out deep feelings and can, strangely, help us to feel better.

6. Conclude by inviting the children to consider how to respond when tears flow. More than a tissue may be needed – although that can help! A friend could simply sit quietly beside someone who is upset. They may need to wait patiently if that person wants to be alone. A word of comfort or encouragement might help – or simply a reassuring touch. Someone who is upset is often helped if someone else

will just listen, not commenting or giving advice. Stress that if the children are ever worried someone is badly hurt or in danger they should tell an adult whom they can trust. Friends share laughter, they share sadness – all times when tears flow.

 Time for reflection

The Bible says that 'Jesus wept'. His tears flowed after the brother of his friends, Martha and Mary, had died (John 11.35). He also shed tears of sorrow and frustration when people didn't understand (Luke 19.41). Jesus knew the deep feelings that make tears flow.

> *Prayer*
> Loving God,
> You are with us . . .
> in happiness and at times of sadness, too.
> Thank you for the gift of tears and for the healing that they bring.
> Help us to be friends who comfort, care and understand.
> **Amen.**

 Songs

'Make me a channel of your peace' (*Come and Praise*, 147)

'He'll be there' (*Songs for Every Assembly*, Out of the Ark Music, 1999)

INDEX OF SUBJECTS AND BIBLICAL REFERENCES

manger 23
marathon 4, 5
Martha (and Mary) 82, 100
Mary 25, 26, 29, 30, 32, 39, 51
mistakes 45, 46, 92
misunderstanding 16, 45
Mohr, Fr Joseph 28
mood 12, 80; *see also* emotions;
   feelings
Mount of Olives 48
movement 93
mustard seed 85
myrrh 32

name, being called by 52
nature 8
Nazareth 35
new beginning 52, 53, 85
new class 73
new school 73
new school year 4, 5
new term 5, 33
New Testament 37
New Year 32
New York 5
Newton, John 37
night 22
Noah 6
nose 24, 93

older person 39
Olympic Games 87
Olympic team 87

painting 80
Palm Sunday 48
pancakes 42, 44
parable 8
parties 24
patience 85
Paul, St 5, 37
peace 13, 18, 23, 29, 49, 59,
   77, 95
Pentecost 58, 67
perseverance 4, 5
Peter, St 62
plants 8, 98
potential 5, 84
practice 5
problem, solving a 30
protest 15

rabbits 53
race (running) 4, 5
rain 97
rainbow 6, 99

referee 58
refugee 34, 36
reindeer 24
remembrance 18, 87
respect 46
resurrection 53
reward 27
river 73, 97
RNLI 71
robin 26
roots 8, 55
Rudolph 24
rules 58

saying sorry 44
Sea Sunday 71
seaside 71
Second World War 14, 18
seed 7, 8, 55
self-restraint 91
senses 97
sheep 22
shepherds 22
Shrove Tuesday 42, 44
silence 18
'Silent night' 28
soil 8, 9, 10, 55, 97; *see also*
   earth
solving a problem 30
sorry *see* saying sorry
souvenirs 71
spider 34, 89
Spirit *see* Holy Spirit
sport 87
stable 23, 26, 29, 35
star 23, 32
stealing 92
storm 13
sower 8
support 33, 87

team 46, 79, 87
tears 45, 52, 99
temple (Jerusalem) 46
temptation 91
tenacity 59
test of character 59
thanks 78
thoughtfulness 91
thoughtlessness 45
tomb 53, 55
tradition 38, 44
traffic lights 65
trouble 92
truce 17; *see also* Christmas
   truce

trust 92
Twelfth Night 34

uncomfortable 22
understanding 73

vegetables 8, 10
vitamins 6

waiting patiently 65
walking 69, 97
wall *see* Berlin Wall
war *see* First World War; Gulf
   War; Second World War
weapons 17
web 35
wedding 30
wheat 8
wheelchair athletes 5
wilderness 46
wine 30, 31
wise men 32, 34
wish 20
wonder 29
world 6, 20, 42, 46, 72

Biblical references
Genesis 8.22 6–7
Psalm 46.10 18
Matthew 4.1–11 46
Matthew 5.9 95
Matthew 13 84
Matthew 28.1–9 53
Matthew 28.16–20 63
Matthew 28.20 74
Luke 2.8–16 22
Luke 2.14 25
Luke 8 12
Luke 19.41 100
Luke 24.13–32 70
John 2 30
John 11.28–29, 31–36 99
John 11.35 100
John 15.26 68
John 20.11–18 51
John 20.19–21 58
John 20.21 60
John 21.1–14 61
Acts 1.1–9 65
Acts 2.42, 44 67, 68
1 Corinthians 12.14–20 93
2 Corinthians 4.8–9, 16 88
Galatians 5.22–23 77
Ephesians 1.16 79
Ephesians 2.14 15
2 Timothy 4.7 4–5